Saint Mirin

GROUND PLAN OF SAINT MIRIN DISTRICT OF ANCIENT AND MODERN PAISLEY,

FOR ILLUSTRATING THE LECTURES.

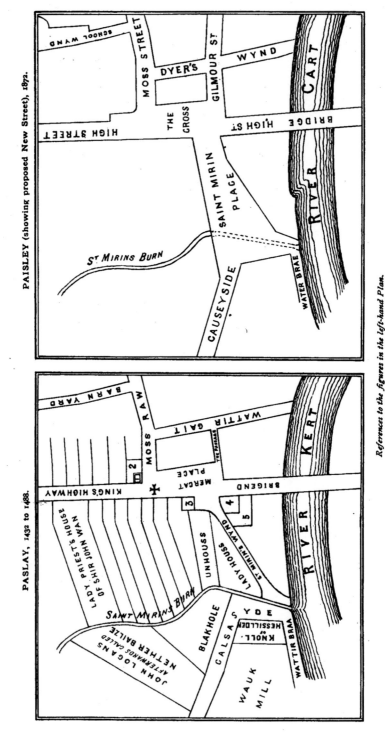

PASLAY, 1432 to 1488.

PAISLEY (showing proposed New Street), 1872.

References to the figures in the left-hand Plan.

1. The Spire or Steeple.   2. The Common Hall   3. The Paslay Tak.   4. The Chamberlain's Houss.   5. Saint Catherine's Tile Tenement.

Saint Mirin:

An Historical Account of
Old Houses, Old Families, and Olden Times,

in Paisley,

being Four Lectures on the Tenements of
**Ladyhouss, Blakhole, Unhouss,
and Paslay Tak,**

in the new line of street from
Cross to Causeyside.

1872

David Semple

Glasgow
The Grimsay Press
2003

The Grimsay Press
an imprint of
Zeticula
57 St Vincent Crescent
Glasgow
G3 8NQ

http://www.thegrimsaypress.co.uk
admin@thegrimsaypress.co.uk

Transferred to digital printing in 2003

First published in Great Britain in 1872 by J. and J. Cook, Paisley.

ISBN 0 902664 75 1

Reproduced from the copy in the Library of the University of Paisley, Scotland

PREFACE.

I N preparing the following Lectures, as a member of the Paisley
Philosophical Society, I had no idea at the time that they would
afterwards be published in a volume, as the "First Series on the
Antiquities of Renfrewshire." The Publishers, who have thought
proper to put them into that convenient and permanent form,
consider the book should have a preface, according to use and
wont, and have asked me to furnish one.

These Lectures were delivered in the Lecture Hall of the Paisley
Free Public Library and Museum, on the 1st, 8th, 15th, and 22nd
March, 1872, and were periodically printed weekly in the columns
of the *Paisley & Renfrewshire Gazette* newspaper, commencing on
9th March, and ending on 13th July, 1872,—nineteen Saturdays.
They contain a history of the old places in Paisley, called Ladyhouss, Blakhole, Unhouss, and Paslay Tak, through which a new
street is to be made from the Cross to Causeyside. The principal
parts of the Charters of these tenements are given in the contracted
or abbreviated Latin words in which they were written, and an
English translation is added. In tracing the history down from
1432, I have taken notice of Saint Mirin, Abbots John de Lithgow
and George Schaw, besides a long list of proprietors and other
persons in the times in which they lived. Saint Mirin's burn has
been described ; and also the rare Gold Lion of King James I.,
found on the banks of the sainted stream. The erection and
destruction of the market cross of Paisley. The litigation between
the Burgh of Renfrew and Burgh of Paisley, and several other law-
suits that have occurred between the owners of the properties. The
Fair and Market Days, with their several alterations. Manufactures
of the town, and occasionally the population of the burgh. The

old chairs of Town-clerk Alexander, of 1629 and 1634, preserved at Ballochmyle; and the Dutch Bell of the Cross Steeple of 1648, old relics of these periods. The local heroes of the Covenanting times. The forgeries of Bailie Maxwell, and the extortions of Sheriff Montgomerie. The great fire of 1733; the rebellion of 1745; the tax on ale for deepening the river Cart; the several attempts made to form the intended street; and a long list of other interesting events, almost embracing a history of Paisley, too tedious to mention in detail, but which are briefly given in the copious Index. In stating the historical facts, I have fortified them with names and dates. However satisfactory these are to readers, it was a very difficult matter to entertwine them with each other in harmony. In naming many of the persons, I have also given their ages, which afford data for calculating the time of events occurring in their lives, and also shows the advanced years great numbers of them attained, and the consequent healthiness of the town where they passed so many days.

It seems to be the invariable custom of all historians of Paisley to quote the inscriptions on the memorial tablets of Abbot JOHN DE LITHGOW of 1433, and of Abbot GEORGE SCHAW of 1485. I followed that good old rule. I have now seen the latter inscription quoted upwards of fifty times, by different persons, and, strange to say, have only observed it in one instance given literally and correctly. Some of the quotations are more accurately executed than others; and the first and worst of them all is that of the historian, George Crawfurd. Words or letters have been erroneously given by subsequent authors. My rendering of the fifth line is, however, different from all others, and therefore requires a word of explanation. This is the third occasion on which I have published it, and it will be eleven years since I first adopted it in that manner. That fifth line had been erased at some period, but I cannot discover the actual year when the act of vandalism was perpetrated. In the year 1636, seventy-six years after the Reformation, the Presbytery of Paisley ordered the remaining monuments of idolatry about the Abbey to be removed; and I suppose that an excited Presbyterian zealot extended his ruthless hand to the, in his mind, offensive prayer contained in the fifth line, and chiselled it off. In perusing the inscription as quoted by former historians, I have always stumbled on arriving at the *limping* measure of that line, compared with the meter of the other lines. I have carefully examined and compared the original inscription, with the view of giving a true and literal copy of the remaining lines, and supplying the evident defect in the fifth line. The inscription stone tablet is five feet three inches in length, and two feet six inches in breadth, and forms the lintel of the passage in the house No. 18 Lawn Street, Paisley. The first line is four feet seven inches long, and a *shield* containing *three covered cups*, the armorial bearings of *Shaw.* The second line, five feet one inch long, and an ornament. The third line, four feet eleven inches, and an ornament. The fourth line, five feet two inches. The fifth line, four feet six inches, and an ornament of a *sprig.* And the sixth line, five feet two inches. The letters are in Saxon character, three-and-a-half inches deep, and all cut in *alto relievo.* The following is the result :—

> Ha callit ye abbot georg of schawe .
> about yis abbay gart make yis waw :
> A thousande four hundereth zeyr
> Auchty ande fywe the date but weir
> Pray for his saulis salbacioun
> Yat made thus nobil fundacioun

In the fifth line, I have supplied the word *saulis* to fill up the space, not only of the whole of the erased line, but also the measure or meter. Fortunately, the vandal who destroyed the line left the original *sprig* at the end of it, which was not offensive in his sight. In measuring the erased space to the sprig, it will take the length of the word *saulis*, or a word of similar length, to be added to fill it up. The following is the inscription, in similar type, quoted by George Crawfurd in 1710, in his "History of Renfrewshire":—

> "*Thy calit the Abbot* George *of* Shaw,
> *About my Abby gart make this Waw,*
> *An thousand four hundreth Zear,*
> *Eighty four the Date but weir ;*
> *Pray for his Salvation*
> *That laid this noble Fundation.*"

The difference of words and orthography in the two inscriptions is at once discernible. The chief blunders in the inscription given by Crawfurd, which can be detected at the present time, in comparing it with the original itself, are the following :—The first word of the first line is "Thy," instead of *They.* In the second line "my" has been substituted for *yis* (this). In the third line, "An" for *A.* In the fourth line, the word "ande" has been omitted, and the word "four" has been substituted for *fywe.* The data for the fifth line has been erased. In the sixth line, the word "laid" has been substituted for *made.* Besides, there are fifteen other errors in the orthography of the other words ; and although these orthographical errors may be considered by some trivial, yet they betray so great a want of accuracy on the part of the historian, that his version cannot be depended on. Every line that is extant shows an egregious blunder, and it is probable the fifth line had a blunder likewise. "Pray for his salvation" will not fill up the *erased* part on the stone. Crawfurd, however, does not say he saw the inscription, but merely that that quotation of his was the inscription. It may have been obtained from hearsay, from the numerous blunders that have been detected. At the present time, there are no such words as "my" in the second line, "an," and "four," in the third line, or "laid" in the last line, inscribed on the stone.

The same historian, in his "Lives of the Officers of State," published in 1726, gives another version of the inscription, printed in similar type, as follows :—

> *They calit the Abbot George of Schaw,*
> *About my Abbey gart mack this Waw,*
> *A thousand foure hundreth Zeir,*
> *Eighti four the Date but weir ;*
> *Pray for his Salvatione*
> *That laid this noble Fundation.*

Subsequent historians, although they corrected several of Crawfurd's errors, continued several of his blunders. The only correct copy of the remaining true inscription on the Tablet will be found in an engraving in the Maitland Club publication, in 1831, of "Hamilton's Description of Lanark and Renfrew." In showing the erasure of the fifth line, however, the original "sprig" at the end of it is also shown to be erased, although it is on the stone at the present time.

"Pray for his soul's salvation" is the usual and common prayer requested to be made by the devout and faithful, for a person that had performed a meritorious work for the Church, such as bestowing lands on the Monastery, or erecting buildings. The following donations to the Monastery of Paisley will show the expression. Charter by Walter Hose, in 1177, of the Church of Craigie, "*pro salute anime mee,*" for my soul's salvation. Charter by Walter, 6th High Steward of Scotland, in 1318, of the Church of Largs, "*pro salute anime mee et marjorie quondam spouse mee,*" for the salvation of the souls of me and Marjory my deceased spouse. Charter by Hugh Wallace of the lands of Thornley, in 1403, "*pro salute anime mei ipsius,*" for the salvation of the soul of myself. Or the prayers on ancient Tombstones, "*Orate pro anime eius;*" or "*Orate pro salute anime eius,*" Pray for his soul, or Pray for his soul's salvation. William Semple, the continuator of Crawfurd, writing in 1782, took it for granted that his predecessor had seen and given a true copy of the inscription, and that the fifth line, "Pray for his salvation," was erased between 1710 and 1735, as he had been informed. There is no use in pursuing that common prayer used in those days, "Pray for his soul's salvation," any further. The erased length and measure of the line requires to be filled up by some word; and I am inclined to ascribe the blunder of omitting the spirit of the whole inscription, to the Presbyterian historian Crawfurd, rather than to the learned Catholic Abbot George Schaw.

I have now performed my duty as a member of the Antiquities Section Committee of the Philosophical Society, in contributing these Lectures for that department of the Institution. In treating of the several topics comprised in these Lectures, I have endeavoured to render them both truthful and interesting, and, from the amount of searching investigation bestowed in elucidation of the various subjects, they will in a great measure place the volume in the position of a future book of reference on local matters.

D. S.

TOWNHEAD,
PAISLEY, *21st August, 1872.*

PAISLEY PHILOSOPHICAL SOCIETY.

SESSION 1871 - 72.

ANTIQUITIES SECTION COMMITTEE.—Messrs. James Caldwell, John Fullerton, J. J. Lamb, A. R. Pollock, Dr. Daniel Richmond, and David Semple; Mr. Lamb, *Convener.*

Excerpt from the Supplementary Report to the Sixty-third Annual Report of the Paisley Philosophical Society, unanimously adopted at a Meeting held on 9th April, 1872.

"PAPERS ON PAISLEY ANTIQUITIES.—The interest in the proper work of the Society had been increased by the Series of Papers which Mr. DAVID SEMPLE had read on Paisley Antiquities. Mr. SEMPLE's enthusiasm as an Antiquarian, the many years which he had devoted to the study of the earliest MSS. connected with the origin and progress of the town, and the thorough reliableness of his statements, gave more than local value to his papers. The information given was, in many instances, extremely curious, and shed light not only on the tastes and social habits of the people at distinct intervals, but on important ecclesiastical and political changes. Early connections between Paisley and other Scottish towns had been indicated in such unexpected ways as must interest antiquarians elsewhere, and a very natural desire had been expressed by those who had heard these papers that they be printed. It had been accordingly resolved that they be published as a 'First Series on the Antiquities of Renfrewshire,' and they trusted that a second series would soon follow, worthy of the admirable commencement which had been made by Mr. SEMPLE. They had in view, also, preparation of a Series of Papers on the Natural History of Renfrewshire. This would, of course, occupy time, and tax several hands; but it would be not only in keeping with the objects for which this Institution had been founded and equipped, but it would be interesting and instructive to the Members of the Society."

Chairmen at the following Lectures.

First Lecture,..................JAMES JAMIESON LAMB, Esq.
Second Lecture,...............ALEX. RUSSELL POLLOCK, Esq.
Third Lecture, ...JAMES CALDWELL, Esq.
Fourth Lecture, ...Rev. WM. FRASER, *President.*

OPENING OF A NEW STREET

FROM THE

CROSS TO CAUSEYSIDE, PAISLEY,

AND

𝕳istory of the 𝕺ld 𝕻laces on the Line of Street.

HE long-cherished improvement of making a spacious street, from the ancient market-place of Paisley, to the old mart of manufactures in Causeyside, will soon be accomplished ; and I now take the opportunity of referring to the efforts that have taken place, to obtain that desirable object, and of giving a history of the old buildings necessary to be taken down. About the end of last century, the population of the Burgh was fast increasing, and the town rapidly extending, in the building of houses. Proposals had been made for improving old streets and opening new ones in the centre of the town ; and these improvements could not be effected without the aid of an Act of Parliament with compulsory powers.

On Friday, the 11th of July, 1806, the statute 46 George III., cap. 116, was passed, commonly called the Paisley Police Act. By the 70th section of that statute, provision was, *inter alia*, made to open a new street from the Cross to Causeyside, to be carried in a line with Moss-street, through the properties No 9 High-street and 115 Causeyside-street. At that period the population of Paisley was 27,934. The expense of purchasing these properties, and taxing the inhabitants, deterred the Police Commissioners

Improvement from the Cross to Causeyside.

Paisley Police Act.

B

from carrying the several improvements contemplated by the Act into execution. In 1823, when the population had increased to 40,039, Mr. Wm. Barr, writer in Paisley, came forward as the vindicator of street improvement, and published a printed memorial on the subject, in which he said—"It is truly lamentable to think that "nothing more of these new streets is visible to "the public but the interesting perspective which "the Act of Parliament affords." Further on he remarked—"the most remarkable of these im-"provements was *an opening from the Cross to* "*Causeyside.* Nothing could be more important "to the town in point of beauty and utility; and, "either in the hands of the Commissioners or of "private persons with Parliamentary powers, it "must have proved even lucrative as well as "useful. While nothing, therefore, should have "prevented the completion of so desirable an "object, yet at this moment operations are in "progress calculated to spoil this for ever, with-"out a murmur on the subject!" Mr. Barr, at that period, was the knight-errant of Burgh reform in Paisley, and he took active measures for securing his election as a Commissioner of Police, in which he was successful. The operations in progress alluded to by Mr. Barr were the taking down of an old house in Causeyside, in the line of the proposed street, and the intended erection of an expensive three-storey tenement on the site. Mr. Barr, on entering the Police Board, did not allow the matter to sleep, but brought forward his street improvement scheme at the very first meeting. He was unsuccessful with his Cross and Causeyside opening—his chief improvement; but carried those for the widening of School-wynd and head of Causeyside, and the opening of the east end of George-street, after a severe and arduous struggle.

Remarks of Mr. William Barr, writer.

Mr. Barr elected Commissioner of Police.

At the time that Mr. Barr was prosecuting his canvass for Commissioner of Police, for the purpose of promoting his beloved scheme of street improvements, particularly from the Cross to Causeyside, he became aware that several influential individuals were averse to the Commissioners of Police interfering in the matter, and had suggested the propriety of effecting it by a joint-stock company. Mr. Barr took the hint, and called a public meeting of all persons interested in the proposed new street from Cross to Causeyside, which was held in the Saracen's Head Inn, on 27th October, 1823, to form a Building Society, to open the thoroughfare in the meantime, and complete the plan in seven years. A committee was appointed to obtain the opinion of six practical tradesmen valuators, and they reported to another meeting, held on 4th November following, that a practicable line of street could be made through Nos. 8, 9, and 10 High-street, and 114 and 115 Causeyside, which would be of incalculable importance to the public, and ornamental to the town ; and the projected speculation, in regard to purchasing and building, would be safe and advantageous. The society was to consist of 200 members, in shares of £100, payable £5 at entry, and £2 monthly thereafter, to raise a capital of £20,000. Only three persons having subscribed £700, the society was not constituted, and the proposed street abandoned.

On Tuesday afternoon, 12th November, 1833, a fire occurred in the warehouse of James Symington, silk mercer, in the four-storey tenement No. 7 Cross, which very quickly laid the whole building in ashes. The fire communicated to the adjoining property, No. 8, which was also burned to the ground. The fire next took hold of the property No. 9 High-street, which shared the fate of the other two. One of the firemen was

Meetings to form a Joint-Stock Company for Improvement.

Fire at the Cross in 1833.

Revival of the Street Improvement.

Prospectus of a Joint-Stock Company to form street.

Orthography of Saint Mirin-street.

killed by the falling walls. All these properties had been built in 1734 and 1735 (after the great fire in the year 1733), in the Flemish style of architecture, and the lurid glare among the crawstepped gables of these buildings, and the reflection of the fire on the old Cross steeple, had a very picturesque appearance. The formation of the intended street was again revived by thirty-three gentlemen (one of whom, Mr. Hodge, Town-Clerk, is the only survivor) sending a requisition to Provost Hardie,—the first Provost elected (on 8th November, 1833) after the passing of the Burgh Reform Act. The Provost called a public meeting, and several meetings of the public and Commissioners of Police were held, and it was proposed to form the street through No. 9 High-street and 114 Causeyside, or from Gilmour-street to Causeyside, through 14 Saint Mirren's-street* and 116 Causeyside ; but it was ultimately resolved not to proceed, and thereby save taxation of the inhabitants. On 13th Feb., 1834, another public meeting was called and held, for the purpose of forming a joint-stock company to make a better opening into Causeyside from the Cross, and it was proposed to purchase the houses on the west side of St. Mirrenstreet, take them down, and widen the wynd into a spacious opening ; but that also failed.

In 1845, the year of railway mania and wild speculations in joint-stock companies for every

---

* The old and proper orthography is Saint *Mirin*, and the modern corrupted mode of spelling is Saint Mirren. The former is the name of a man, and the corruption makes it the Scots name for a woman. John Tait, the publisher of the first Glasgow Directory, in 1783, including Paisley, uses the English name for a woman, and prints Saint *Marion's*-wynd. Wherever the name *Mirren* appears, that is the name that has been improperly used in modern times in reference to the wynd or street.

conceivable object, a new scheme for making a more accessible thoroughfare from the Cross to Causeyside was laid before the community. It was headed,—"Prospectus of a new Joint-Stock "Company or Improvement and Building Society "in Paisley. Capital, £50,000 ; or 5000 shares "of £10 each." The prospectus stated that St. Mirren's-wynd was narrow, steep, and dangerous, and then referred to the Police Act having made provision for a new thoroughfare. The promoters then proposed to form a company, who, with concurrence of the Commissioners of Police, under their Act of Parliament, or with a new Act, to make the new street, with lateral branches into the Laigh Kirk-lane and New-street, and they concluded by saying that the extensive frontage towards the new proposed streets, for the erection of handsome shops and warehouses, would prove a safe and lucrative investment. At that time the kingdom had become a nation of monomaniacs, who were insanely rushing forward with applications for shares in every reckless speculation having the name of railway or joint-stock company, excepting the safe and lucrative investment from the Cross to Causeyside. The intelligent and canny bodies of Paisley did not patronise the new scheme, with its lateral branches, and it was withdrawn ; but an investment there would have been much better than some of those made in foreign, worthless projects.

Reckless speculations in the kingdom.

In 1855, ten years afterwards, Mr. David MacDonald, sewed muslin manufacturer, formerly in Paisley, then in Glasgow, next came forward, single-handed, to purchase the houses on the west side of St. Mirren-street, take them down, widen the street, and erect a line of elegant buildings for shops and warehouses for the improvement of his native town. He was looked upon as a

Mr. MacDonald's scheme for improving Saint Mirin's-wynd.

wealthy gentleman, and the credit of his firm was unlimited with the Western Bank of Scotland. He bought a few of the old houses ; but before he could get the remainder purchased, the single-handed improvement failed, from the failure of the house with which he was connected, carrying on business in Glasgow, London, Manchester, Liverpool, Belfast, New York, and Canada, coming down with a tremendous crash in November, 1857, involving liabilities to the enormous amount of £423,535 13s. 1d.

General Police Act, 1862.

On 7th August, 1862, the statute 25th and 26th Victoria, cap. 101, called "The General Police and Improvement (Scotland) Act, 1862," was passed, and partially adopted by the Commissioners of Police for the Burgh of Paisley. On Thursday, 24th March, 1864, a public meeting of the inhabitants was held in the Gaelic Church, when the statute was adopted. The old Commis-

Old Commissioners superseded & Town Council appointed.

sioners of Police, under the local Act, were superseded, and the Town Council appointed Commissioners of Police under the General Police and Improvement Act. These new Commissioners of Police commenced their work of improvement in earnest; and when the large four-storey tenement with

Purchase of properties for street.

back buildings, No. 14 Saint Mirren-street, was exposed for public sale on 24th May, 1866, at the upset price of £1500, the Commissioners of Police purchased it at that sum. Immediately afterwards, they acquired, by private contract, the four-storey tenement and *Nepus*, No 116 Causeyside-street, and several of the two-storey houses on the west side of Saint Mirren-street, which were erected after the great fire in 1733, for the purpose of forming the long-projected street from the Cross to Causeyside. In 1871, the Commissioners also acquired, by private bargain, the eastmost half of the tenement, No. 6 High-street, the three-storey tenement, No. 115 Causeyside, and other three of the old houses on the west side of Saint Mirren-street, to increase the width of the street, and finish it off to better advantage.

On Wednesday, 23rd December, 1871, a special meeting of the Commissioners of Police was held, and the Board, after mature deliberation, resolved to open the street from the Cross to Causeyside, after the removal term of Whitsunday next. They also agreed, and immediately carried it out, to warn the tenants of Nos. 13 and 14 Saint Mirren's-street, and 115 and 116 Causeyside-street, to remove at Whitsunday first.

Resolution to open street.

The opening of a new street from the Cross, in continuation of Moss-street to the Causeyside, was obviously the best at the time the Police Act was obtained, sixty-five years ago; but, from other great improvements that have been made upon the town since that period, have rendered the present selected site for the new street the most desirable of the two. These great improvements were the erection of the Coffee-Room Buildings and the County Buildings, and the opening of Gilmour-street and the Railways. The street from the County Buildings to Dyers'-wynd was opened in 1829, after a jury trial with Robert Muir, and was called Gilmour-street, for Provost William Gilmour, by which new street communication was had with the Cross by the ancient "passage" of nine feet wide, afterwards called Lillie's-wynd, and vulgarly, the "Hole o' the wa'." The continuation of Gilmour-street to the Cross, or rather the widening of the ancient Passage or Lillie's-wynd, was effected in 1845. The line of the new and spacious opening for the accommodation of the southern inlets of the town will be made through 115 and 116 Causeyside, and the west side of Saint Mirren-street, to line with Gilmour-street. Gilmour-street has now become

Public buildings in Gilmour-street.

an important thoroughfare, containing the Coffee-Room Buildings, erected in 1809; the Union Bank of Scotland, built in 1846, which is one of the finest buildings in the town for its architecture, material, and workmanship; the British Linen Bank, built in 1867; the Government School of Design, erected in 1847; the castellated County Buildings, the foundation stone of which was laid, with great Masonic pomp and ceremony, on Saturday, 3rd October, 1818; and terminating with the railway stations and the railways, opened to the public on 11th August, 1840, which are now in connection with the whole railway system of Great Britain. Gilmour-street, passing under the Railway Arch, is continued into New Sneddon in a direct line, leading into the north part of the town.

Old and New Plans of District.

With the view of illustrating and explaining my observations, I have prepared and refer the reader to a plan of the village of Paslay, A.D. 1432 to 1488, with the names of all the ancient streets and places at the time; and another plan of the same district for the year 1872, embracing all the recent improvements in that part of the town, and also the spacious opening from the Cross to Causeyside, which I have marked "SAINT MIRIN PLACE." *

Properties to be taken down.

The properties to be taken down being situated in one of the oldest parts of the town, I have considered it a fitting opportunity to give this history before they are entirely swept away. The subject may be very properly divided into four chapters, from the descriptive or designative names. These properties were called in olden times—

    I. "The Lady Houss."   III. "The Unhouss."
    II. "The Blakhole."   IV. "The Paslay Tak."

---

* *See* Frontispiece.

I.

𝕿𝖍𝖊 𝕷𝖆𝖉𝖞 𝕳𝖔𝖚𝖘𝖘.

Now, west side of Saint Mirren's Street.

———

HE road leading from the King's Highway to the Causeyside was originally
called the Common Vennell, and the
west side of it the Lady House and land
of the chaplain who officiated at the altar dedicated
to the blessed Virgin Mary, called the Lady Altar.
The first charter granted for ground on the west
side of the Vennell now in existence, was by Abbot
John Lithgow, in the year 1432, and was, as all
ancient charters generally are, written in Latin, of
which I shall give a copy of the principal portions,
with all the contractions of words, and subjoin an
English translation :—

" *Carta Jhois schelys*

*Vniversis christi fidelibus pnt lras visuris vel audituris
Jhoes de lychquhou misse dia Abbas mostij de pasleto
et eiusd locj convtos. Sltem in dno sepita Novrit uni-
versitas vra nos hito sup hoc pus diligete tractatu utilitate mostij nri prefatate vna concensu et assensu totius
capl nro dedisse conssisse et ad feodifma demississe
Dilecto nro Jhoes de schelis illud tenetm qd dicitr tra
capellanj iacen in villa nra de pasleto int tra quond
thos redheid ex pte occidentalis eiusd ex pte vna et a dta
tra thos redheid continen in frote usqe tra Andree
smyt ex pte orietali sicut coes venella se extendet versus
rivolu sct mirini sexagitu vlnas cu qtis Et a dta tra
adree smyt usq ad dict rivolu continen vigiti septe vlnas
et sic ascendedo sup dtm rivolu ex pte austrli eiusd
usqe ad tra dicti thos redheid et sic ascendendo a dto
sup rivolo ex pte occidetali usq ad limitas int dtm
tenetm et tra Jois Kuk filij continen in se quiquagita*

C

Date. 8th August, 1432.	*tres vlnas et sic ascededo et descededo thos redheid ex vtraqe pte in latitudine et logitudie cum suis mete et se limitate et disis ut sup dtm est* * * * * *In cuj rei testioum sigillu coe capli nri ptibus appensum apud mostum nrm sup dtm octavo die mesis augustj Anno dm milesimo quadragintu trecesimo scdo."*

TRANSLATION.

" Charter of John Sheils.

English translation of charter.	"To all the faithful in Christ who may see or hear the present letter, John of Lychquhou, by divine permission, Abbot of the Monastery of Paisley and convent of the same place : Be it known to you all that we, after diligent inquiry, for the utility of our Monastery foresaid, with one consent and assent of our whole Chapter, have given, granted, and in feu
Description of tenement.	farm let, to our beloved John of Sheils, that tenement which is called the land of the chaplain, lying in our village of Paisley, between the land formerly Thomas Redheid on the west part thereof, and one side ; and from the said land of Thomas Redheid, extending in front as far as the lands of Andrew Smyth on the east part, along the Common Vennell itself, extending towards the rivulet of Saint Mirin sixty and one-fourth ells ; and from the said land of Andrew Smyth to the said rivulet, containing twenty-seven ells ; and so ascending up the said rivulet, on the south part of the same, to the land of the said Thomas Redheid, and so going up from the said rivulet on the west part as far as to the boundary between the said tenement and the land of the son of John Kuk, containing in itself fifty-three ells ; and so going up and down on each side in length and breadth, with their measures, marches, and
Date. 8th August, 1432.	boundaries, as is above set forth * * * * In witness whereof, the common seal of our chapter is hung to these presents, at our Monastery, upon the eighth day of August, in the year of our Lord one thousand four hundred and thirty-two."
Charters best proofs for history.	Of all proofs in history, none are so conclusive and pointed as charters. They contain the truth,

and require no embellishments to persuade ; and
are not, like histories, overgrown with legends of
miracles and visions on the one hand, and interspersed with traditions and fables on the other.
A diligent search among ancient title deeds and
records clears up obscurity, corrects untruths,
and supplies omissions that have occurred in history.

John d'Lychgow, the granter of the charter to
John Shiels, was appointed Abbot of Paisley previous to 1368, when Robert Stewart, 7th High
Steward of Scotland, and Baron of the Barony of
Renfrew (grandson of King Robert Bruce), afterwards King Robert II., was patron of the Monastery
of Paisley. In the first volume of the Chartulary
of Passelet, page 328, there is an Instrument
defining the privileges of our Lord Bishop of
Glasgow, dated 30th January, 1368, in which the
name of the Abbot and two of his monks appear ;
and, from an engraved inscription on a stone
tablet inserted in the inside of the east wall of
the north porch of Paisley Abbey, it appears he
was still Abbot in 1433.

Abbot Lythgow

iohes . d . lychtgw . ab
bas . huius . monastij . xx . die
mesis . januarij . ano . dm . m°. cccc°
xxxiij . Elegit . sexi . sua . sepultura

Inscription in north porch of Abbey.

"*John of Lychtgow, abbot of this monastery
made choice of his burial place the xx day of the
month of January MCCCCXXXIII.*"

An Abbot must be twenty-five years of age at
his election, and Abbot Lychtgow was perhaps
older before he attained that dignity, and would
be ninety-five years of age when he selected his
place of sepulture in the Monastery. The seal
of the Abbot was of an oblong shape, and contained the image of the Abbot, in the attitude of
celebrating at the altar, holding a pastoral staff

Abbot Lycht-gow's seal.

in his hand, and on the circumference was inscribed the words,

" **Sigillum Abbatis Monasterij de Passelet**,"

"The Seal of the Abbot of the Monastery of Paisley."

Queen Blearie's tomb.

The altar-tomb in Saint Mirren's Aisle, vulgarly called Queen Blearie's tomb, has the name Abbot Lychtgow engraved over two of the representations on the left side of the tomb. George Crawfurd, in his "History of Renfrewshire," writing in 1710, says, "There is a monu-"ment erected to the memory of Marjory Bruce, "daughter of the renowned King Robert I., "mother of King Robert II., and in the form of a "woman raised about two feet above the surface of "the ground, and is called Queen Blearie's "tomb." The same George Crawfurd, in his "Lives of the Officers of State," published in 1726, says, "Abbot George Schaw died in 1504, "and was buried in the Isle adjoining to the

Abbot Schaw's monument.

"Abbey Church, where his funeral monument is "yet to be seen." William Semple, the continuator of the history, writing in 1782, page 292, says, "Marjory Bruce died in 1317, and she "lies buried at Paisley, where is a monument to "her memory—vizt., now on the north side, and "near to the west end of this burial-place or "Sounding Aisle. In the yard you may see a "stone, with three coats of arms upon it,—vizt., "*Paisley Coat of Arms*, the Pope of Rome's, and "another I do not know." As I will require to

William Semple's history.

refer to William Semple's history on several occasions, I consider it proper to explain that I am not related to him. He belonged to the Cartside family of Semples, and I belong to the Middleton family of Semples. The "Paisley

Paisley Coat of Arms.

Coat of Arms" referred to by Semple is a shield with a fess cheque and three roses,—one in *dexter* chief, a second in *sinister* chief, and the third in middle base. In front of the original Grammar School of Paisley, erected on the tenement of the chaplain of Saint Ninian, on the south side of School-wynd, now No. 4 thereof, there was a tablet, with the inscription,

"𝔗𝔥𝔢 𝔊𝔯𝔞𝔪𝔞𝔯 𝔖𝔠𝔥𝔦𝔩, 1586,"

Grammar School.

with similar coat of arms, and on the right and left side of the arms the initials 𝔒.𝔓., for "𝔒𝔭𝔭𝔱𝔲𝔲𝔪 𝔓𝔞𝔰𝔩𝔢𝔱𝔢𝔪," — *the Town of Paisley.* When the original school was taken down in 1753, the stone tablet was put into the new building. On the newer Grammar School being erected in Church-hill, in 1802, the tablet was put up there. And on the newest Grammar School and Academy being erected in Oakshaw-street, in 1863, the tablet was transferred from the previous building to the new Grammar School and Academy. Semple, again, at page 513, says the Town of Paisley's coat of arms is engraved in front of the meal market, with the date 1665. That armorial stone is now in the Free Museum, where it can be seen, and the fess cheque and three roses are similarly placed. On a communion token of the Laigh Church, inscribed "PASLEY TOUN, 1739," the same arms appear, — a fess cheque and three roses placed in a similar position as the other three. In forty-five years afterwards, a new issue of tokens was made, with the inscription and date, "PAISLEY TOWN, 1784," and containing the same armorial bearings. These were the simple arms of the Burgh adopted up to that date. Semple, writing in 1782, page 318, says :—"Arms "of the Town of Paisley, *or*, a fess cheque, *sable*, "between three seals, *gules*, wreathed about the "shield with two—stalked and leaved *vert* fructed "*gules*, *i.e.*,—bearing fruit." William Semple also published a plan of Paisley in 1782, on which is engraved the coat of arms that he has described,

Meal market.

Laigh Church tokens.

William Semple's Plan of Paisley.

Present seal of the Burgh of Paisley.

—a wreathed shield, containing the fess cheque, with three roses the same as in the others. The common seal of the Burgh at present used has a figure representing Abbot George Schaw, founder of the Burgh, standing on a shield, with three covered cups, the arms of Schaw; on the right side, a shield with fess cheque; on the left, a shield with two roses in chief, and an escallop shell in base, with a tree behind, eradiated and fructed; and around the margin an inscription,—

" SIGILLUM · COMMUNE · BURGI · DE · PAISLEY "

"The Common Seal of the Burgh of Paisley."

The letters are all Roman capitals, and the word *Paisley* not being Latinised, and given in modern orthography, bears evidence of its modern make. The present seal or coat of arms of the Burgh, so tastefully designed and well executed, must have been adopted since 1784, and is not ninety years old. The Paisley new coat of arms, beautifully cut in *alto relievo*, has been placed in front of the present Grammar School, with an inscription below,—

New Heraldic Arms on Grammar School.

" 𝔍𝔞𝔟 · 𝔍𝔞𝔠 · 𝔡𝔦 · 𝔰 ℜ · 𝔐𝔟𝔩𝔵𝔵𝔳𝔦."

Dr. Boog's account of Queen Blearie's tomb.

The Rev. Dr. Robert Boog, who was inducted one of the ministers of the Abbey on 21st April, 1774, wrote an account of Queen Blearie's tomb in 1821, which is printed in the " Transactions of the Society of the Antiquaries of Scotland," Vol. II.,

p. 456. He says that in the centre of the lower area of the chapel stood what was called "Queen Blearie's Tomb." It retained its original situation till 1715, when John, fourth Earl of Dundonald, removed it to a corner of the Abbey gardens, where it was rebuilt in its original form : that Thomas, eighth Earl of Dundonald, resolving to feu that part of the garden, had the monument again taken down, removed, and the stones were thrown aside and forgotten. Dr. Boog says he was fourteen years in Paisley before he knew that such a monument had existed, or that its materials might possibly be discovered. In 1789, the Abbey Church underwent a complete repair, and in removing accumulated masses of rubbish in different places, the stones which formed the monument were found, and were loosely, but carefully, put together in the Cloister Court. These were again removed by Dr. Boog in 1817, and ingeniously erected in their present position in Saint Mirren's Aisle, vulgarly called the Sounding Aisle, and now form an interesting object to visitors—to hear the echo which, Pennant says, is one of the finest in the world.

In taking a view of the altar-tomb at the present day, we see that the stone with Paisley Coat of Arms has been placed at the head, the stones with the ecclesiastics in compartments at the sides, and the female figure on the top. There are nine full compartments of an oblong or oval form, and a one-half compartment at each end. The foot of the altar-tomb has been supplied with a stone with empty compartments. On the right side, No. 1 compartment is filled with a Bishop holding in his hand a crozier ; No. 4, a Bishop at prayer,—and, that no mistake may afterwards occur with this representation, his name is engraved on a scroll, roбᴇrt ᴡꝑꙅꜧarꝺ. On the left side, No. 1 compartment is filled with the image

[margin note: Position of Altar-Tomb in Sounding Aisle.]

[margin note: Robert Wyshard, Bishop of Glasgow.]

Abbot Lychtgow.

of an Abbot in the attitude of celebrating at the altar, holding a pastoral staff in his left hand, and on a scroll his name is inscribed johes d. lychtgw; and in No. 4, the image of an Abbot at prayer,— and, that there be no mistake, his name, johes d. lychtgw, is given again. Nos. 3, 6, 7, and 9, on both sides, are filled with monks in the attitude of prayer, and all the other compartments are empty. Bishop Robert Wishart, of Glasgow, was the bosom friend of King Robert Bruce, and the greatest Scots statesman of that age, and co-prisoner in England with Marjory Bruce, the King's daughter, afterwards the wife of Walter, sixth High Steward. Both the princess and the prelate died in 1316, and Abbot John Lithgow in 1433 or 1434. The village of Paisley was erected into a Burgh in 1488, and Saint Mirin's Aisle was not finished till after 1499. Many changes would occur between 1316 and the Re-formation, or Church Revolution of 1560. Many a monument would be cast down, broken, and thrown aside; and these few monumental relics of

Relics in the Sounding Aisle.

Paisley Monastery, collected in the Sounding Aisle and ingeniously fitted together, had even several removals between 1714 and 1818. There is no evidence that the whole stones belonged originally to one monument, and they may have been parts of three or four different monuments, —the female figure belonging to one period, the two sides to one or two periods, and the arms or head-stone to a third period. I am principally directing attention to Abbot Lytchgw, the granter of the charter, and will not make many conjec-tures about these several periods. The left side of the monument is evidently connected with that Abbot, when his image is twice represented, and his name twice repeated. It may have been one side of his own monument, and either been sculptured during his lifetime or after his death, in imitation of the right side or part of Robert Wishart's monument, the Bishop of the diocese; but most probably the former.   Abbot Lithgow must have had a taste for the fine arts and stone inscriptions, and may have been taught sculpture, and exercised the art as part of his secular duties for adorning the church.   He had his image engraved on his seal, his name is engraved on the stone tablet in the north porch, and his image and name appear twice on the altar-tomb.   Of all the thirteen Abbots of Paisley Monastery, his name is the only name that is to be seen on the buildings, and that thrice repeated.   The sound of the Abbot's name brings to my recollection the name of John Lithqu, the stone engraver who was employed to make the lettering around the tomb erected in 1329, in the Cathedral Church of Dunfermline, to our Lord King Robert Bruce. The Abbot was probably the grandson of the engraver, and was probably taught the art of stone-engraving and sculpture—memorials of which, particularly of the former, I presume, have remained in Paisley Abbey for at least 438 years, as sharp as when the chisel left them.   The patron of the Abbey was the grandson of the King, and the Abbot may have been the grandson of the engraver of the King's tomb, and, from that connection, appointed Abbot of Paisley in 1368.

John Lithqu, stone engraver.

The next individual is the vassal, John de Schelis.   This is the only occasion that the name appears; but whether the second name was the name of his estate, or had then become a surname, there is no means of knowing.   In 1505, this property belonged to Marion Schelis, probably a grand-daughter of John of Sheils.   In 1510, a Patrick Schelis became proprietor of a tenement in the mustard-yard at the head of Causeyside.

John of Sheils, vassal of the tenement.

The property is described as bounded by the lands formerly belonging to Thom Redheid, on

Boundaries of tenement.

D

the north,—a name in all probability given to him, or that of his ancestor, from the carroty adornment of his caput,—and the lands of Andrew Smyth on the south, a very common name. These parties must have been rental tenants of the Abbey. The only rental book in existence commences on the last day of April, 1460. The property extended along the common vennel on the one side, and the rivulet of Saint Mirin on the other.

The common vennel in these days was a narrow, steep road, crossing the burn by a ford, and at that time the surface of the road at the burn was seven feet lower than it is at the present day, and the ground on the opposite side of Causeyside from the burn was originally called the "Knoll," from its height, and afterwards "Hassilden." The common vennel has also borne successively the names, — Saint Mirin's-vennel, Saint Mirin's-wynd, the Burngait, Water-wynd, and Saint Mirren's-street. The first time the prefix, "Saint Mirin," appears to this roadway is in the charter of John Stewart, granted in 1505, to be afterwards noticed, and was probably conferred from the name of the rivulet. The road or street is 270 feet in length, and 16 feet in breadth.

The Rivulet—the natural boundary on the south—has received a very dignified name for such an insignificant stream,—the name of the tutelar Saint of Paisley, Saint Mirin. The streamlet rises in the lands of Wellmeadow and West Over Common, and flows about half a mile between the lands of Priorscroft and the village of Passeleth, on the north; and the lands of East Over Common, Causeyside, and Black-hole, on the south; and then falls into the River Cart. The village of Passeleth extended from the River Cart along the King's highway, now High-street,

Marginal notes:

Various Names of the vennel or wynd.

Rivulet of Saint Mirin.

to Priorscroft,—or No. 17 High-street, on the south side, and 93 High-street on the north side. Priorscroft extended from 17 High-street to the vennel now called Lady-lane, and the lands of Black-hole to those of Causeyside; and those of Causeyside to the East Over Common, now Storie-street; and the lands of East Over Common to the Vennel or Lady-lane.   Priorscroft perhaps obtained the name from its being the croft land assigned to the Prior of the House of Devotion, founded by the High Steward in 1163, which was originally a Priory.   This charter of Abbot Lithgow is the oldest charter in existence containing reference to the rivulet of Saint Mirin, and it will be a matter of speculation when the stream received its name of Saint Mirin.   The stream was probably adopted by Mirin in his wanderings in the West of Scotland, where his sainted name had been conferred on it, and where he performed his miracles.   I will, however, leave to other persons more fertile in imagination than myself, to relate the pensive musings and describe the holy meditations of Mirin on the banks of the rivulet, and the miraculous cures effected from the water of the "Meadow Well," the fountain of Saint Mirin's burn.   My father has repeatedly mentioned to me that the burn was frequented by shoals of minnows, and occasionally visited by the speckled trout; while the water was clear and pure, and daily used for domestic purposes. And it may have been in this very burn that the genteel boy, Master John Wilson, in a real jacket —the embryo Professor Wilson (whose father's mansion was erected on the lands of Priorscroft, the garden of which descended down to the burn) —and with a wand for a rod, a linen thread for a line, and a bended pin for a hook, under the guidance of handy William Hanna, his father's gardener, learned the initiatory lessons in angling,

Priorscroft.

Purity of the water.

Angling of Christopher North.

Pollutions of burn.

carried into practice in the burns and rivulets in the parish of Mearns, and afterwards developed into the Christopher North of *Noctes* celebrity at the Highland lochs, in his sporting jacket.* The first pollutions the limpid stream received were from a brewery erected on the west side of Lady-lane, at the end of the last century; and since that time, pollutions of every description have daily increased, converting the burn into an offensive open common sewer,—an Augean Cloacina.

Saint Mirin the tutelary Saint of Paisley.

Saint Mirin, whose name the rivulet just referred to bears, was the second of the three patron saints to whom the House of Devotion, founded at Paisley, in 1163, was dedicated. Very little is known of the Saint, and what has been handed down is like the life of other saints, chiefly composed of extra-

* Mr. Semple here noticed that, after writing the remarks about Master Wilson's first lessons in angling, he recollected reading, about 40 years ago, an account of it in *Blackwood's Magazine* for October, 1832. He read it as follows :—

Noctes Ambrosianæ.

" JEFFREY.

Come, North, you promised me a song. You're in sweet voice to-night.
     NORTH (Sings).
     AIR—' *The Ploughboy.*'

When I was a mere school-boy, ere yet I'd learned my book,
I felt an itch for angling in every little brook;
An osier rod, some thread for twine, a crooked pin for hook,
And thus equipped I wandered by many a bubbling brook,
Where prickle-backs and minnows each day I caught in store,
With stone-loaches and miller's-thumbs,—such brooks afford
  no more.
     'Twas thus the tiny angler,
       With crooked pin for hook,
     Would shun each noisy wrangler,
       To fish the murmuring brook.

     JEFFREY.

Sweet and simple. Do go on, my dear North, you awaken a thousand long-forgotten dreams of innocence."
       Blackwood's Magazine, vol. 32, p. 724.

Life of Professor Wilson.

He then read from Mrs. Gordon's life of her

ordinary miracles, bordering on the fabulous. In the seven or eight calendars of Scots saints that have been compiled, Saint Mirin is only noticed in two of them. In Adam King's calendar, he is entered, " 15th September, *Saint mirin, abot of* "*paslay, and confess in Scotland, under king* "*finbarmache ;*" and in David Cameron's calendar under " 17th September, *Sanctus Mirinus, Neu-* "*botilensi in Laudonia Scotiæ provincia celebris,*"— "Saint Mirin of Paisley in Scotland, and after- "wards of Newbottle in Lothian in Scotland, re- "nowned in the provinces." Although Saint Mirin's name does not occur in the other half-dozen of calendars, that will not prove he did not exist, but merely shows that these compilers performed their work imperfectly in not discovering him.

Saint Mirin must have been well known to Walter Fitzallan, High Steward of Scotland, first Baron of the Barony of Renfrew, when he dedicated his House of Devotion at Paisley to Saint James, *Saint Mirin*, and Saint Milburge. The High Steward and his advisers would acquire their information either from written history or tradition that could be depended upon, of the Saint having been connected with Paisley at a

Charter of Endowment of Paisley Monastery.

---

father, Professor Wilson, published in 1862, her remarks respecting the angling—

"He (Professor Wilson) was but three years old when he rambled off one day, armed with a willow-wand, duly furnished with a thread line and crooked pin, to fish in a 'wee burnie' of which he had taken note, away a good mile from home."

Vol. I., p. 4.

Mr. Semple said that, after perusing these, he saw no occasion to alter his text ; and that the same William Hanna, who continued gardener with Mr. Sym, Professor Wilson's uncle, and with William Fulton, Esq., who purchased the mansion from Professor Wilson, and resided there, had taught both Master James Fulton and himself to bait crooked pins. The gardener died in June, 1832, aged 69.

William Hanna, successively gardener to Wilson, Sym, and Fulton.

Capitular seals.

former period. The Cluniac monks of Paisley Monastery must also have been versant in the history of the Saint, from the inscription on their common seal. From impressions of seals hung to charters, granted by the abbots and convent, it appears they had used at least two seals. The inscription round the margin of the one side of the older seal is—

𝔖 : 𝕮𝖆𝖕𝖎𝖙𝖇𝖑𝖎 : 𝔖𝖈𝖎 : 𝕴𝖆𝖈𝖔𝖇𝖎 : 𝖊𝖙 : 𝔖𝖈𝖎 : 𝕸𝖎𝖗𝖎𝖓𝖎 : 𝖉𝖊 : 𝕻𝖆𝖘𝖘𝖊𝖑𝖊𝖙𝖔

"The Seal of Saint James and Saint Mirin of Passeleth."

Saint James' seal, obverse.

The figure in the above seal represents Saint James, the apostle, the first patron saint, with a pilgrim's staff and scrip. At each side is a shield, the *dexter* bearing a fess cheque for Stewart; the *sinister*, a saltire, cantoned with four roses, for Arkill of Lennox. Above the right shield is a saltire and crescent, interspersed with sprigs, and above the left shield a saltire and three stars; between the figure and the left shield is a *fleur de lis*, and below it sprigs. The inscription round the margin of the other, or reverse, side of the older seal is—

Saint Mirin's seal, reverse.

𝕏𝖗𝖎𝖘𝖙𝖇𝖒 : 𝖕𝖗𝖔 : 𝖋𝖆𝖒𝖇𝖑𝖎𝖘 : 𝕻𝖔𝖘𝖈𝖊 : 𝕸𝖎𝖗𝖎𝖓𝖊 : 𝕿𝖇𝖎𝖘.

"O Mirin! Pray to Christ for thy servants."

The figure in that shield represents Saint Mirin in the pontifical vestments of a bishop, his right hand raised in prayer, and his left holding a crozier. The same shields on the right and left side of the figure, as on the other side of the seal, with an additional cheque to the fess. Above the right shield is a saltire and crescent, and above the left shield a saltire and star. At the right side of the Saint's head is a *fleur de lis*, and at his feet two sprigs of foliage.

The older seal may have been made either shortly after the foundation of the Monastery, or by Abbot Lithgow, who had a taste for the fine arts. The other or later seal, I think, would be made during the time of Abbot Robert Shaw, between 1498 and 1524. The letters of the inscription are considerably modernised from those in the older seal, and the word "Passeleto" is spelled "Passelet." There are other variations in the details of the seals, which can only be observed on a comparison of the two.

In the legendary histories of Saint Andrews, and the Scotichronicon of John Fordun, written about the year 1386, it is stated that Saint Regulus, carrying with him the relics of Saint Andrew, sailed from Patros in Greece about the year 345, accompanied by several associates, among whom was one called Mirinus. That Saint Regulus founded the church of Saint Andrews; some of the other associates, other churches; and it was supposed Mirinus had been sent on a mission, or wandered to the West of Scotland, and founded a church at Paisley. The writers of these histories, it may be remarked, are recording legends which, according to their account, happened upwards of a thousand years previously. *[margin: Histories of Saint Andrews, and Fordun's Scotichronicon.]*

The next legendary history is the Breviary of Aberdeen, compiled by William Elphinston, elected Bishop of Aberdeen 1484, and who wrote it about that period, makes the date of Saint Regulus sailing about the year 360. The Bishop, *[margin: Breviary of Aberdeen.]*

in noticing Mirinus, does not refer to the Mirinus of Fordun and the Register of Saint Andrews in the 4th century, but to another and different Mirinus in the 6th or 7th centuries, belonging to Ireland. Bishop Elphinston has bestowed considerable labour on his legendary history in his Breviary, and he may have applied to the Abbots of his day to supply him with information respecting the lives of the Patron Saints of their houses, somewhat similar to the manner in which the statistical accounts of Scotland were furnished by the respective ministers of parishes. The abbots, in furnishing these lives, would particularly mention the miracles performed by the saints, those holy men, whom their house had adopted for patrons, however ridiculous, absurd, and fabulous the same may have been. Professor Cosmo Innes, the celebrated antiquary, in his preface to the Chartulary of the Monastery of Passelet, printed by the Earl of Glasgow for presentation to the Maitland Club in 1832, made a quotation from the venerable Breviary respecting Saint Mirin, and I cannot do better than follow the example of such an eminent archæologist, by making a quotation from him :—" Bishop " Elphinston says, that a colony from Wenlock " carried with it to Paisley the same reverence for " its patron saint, and the new Monastery was " dedicated to Saint Milburge, together with " Saint James, the patron of an older church, " where the new monks had first settled, and " Saint Mirinus, bishop and confessor, whose " history also speaks the country of his origin. " This other peculiar patron saint of Paisley, " was educated, says the *Scottish Breviary*, under " Saint Congallus, in the Abbey of Bangour. " Resisting the temptations of wealth and rank to " which he was born, he devoted himself to a " monastic life, and became prior of the Monastery

Chartulary of Passelet.

Professor Cosmo Innes.

Saint Mirinus.

"of Bangour, under the Abbot Congallus. No-
"thing more of his life is added by this apocryphal
"chronicle, except the details of a few of his
"miracles, which are not in general distinguished
"by much originality.   At one time, a holy
"bishop, a guest in the Abbey, requiring milk,
"*propter molliorem sui corporis qualitatem,* when
"there was none in the Monastery, it was
"miraculously supplied by the intervention of
"Mirinus.   On another occasion, he restored, by
"his prayers, one of his brethren who had fallen
"down from extreme labour and thirst, after he
"had lain lifeless for many hours.   A third ex-
"ertion of the Saint's miraculous powers is some-
"what more singular.   Travelling on a religious
"mission, he arrived at the castle of the King of
"Ireland, and prayed to be admitted.   It
"happened that the Queen was then in the pains
"of childbirth,—and on that account, or for other
"reasons, the saint was denied admittance, or
"treated with disrespect, upon which, departing
"in indignation, he entreated of heaven that
"the King might suffer the pains of labour
"instead of his wife.   This fearful malediction
"was immediately fulfilled, so that for three days
"and nights the miserable monarch was heard by
"all the subjects of his kingdom to cry incessantly,
"like a woman in travail, until at length, finding
"all remedies of physicians in vain, he took
"means to appease the saint, and was by him
"delivered from his sufferings.   We are not in-
"formed when Mirinus became a bishop, nor even
"at what time he lived; but the venerable
"*Breviary* states that, full of miracles and
"sanctity, he fell asleep in the Lord at Paisley,
"and the church there was dedicated to his
"honour."

Bishop Elphinston and Abbot George Schaw
were contemporaries.   Bishop Elphinston was

E

[Margin note:] Miracles of Saint Mirin.

[Margin note:] Bishop Elphinston and Abbot Schaw.

made official of Glasgow in 1471; and Abbot Schaw was elected Abbot of Paisley on Saint Peter's day, 29th June, 1472. In seven months thereafter, both of them were witnesses to a charter of Andrew Muirhead, Bishop of Glasgow, confirming the foundation of James Douglas of Auchencassill, sealed at Glasgow, on 29th January, 1472, before George, Abbot of Paisley, and Master William Elphinston, official of Glasgow. The two had frequently met on other occasions. On 31st June, 1493, they met in Edinburgh, at the hearing of a dispute between the bailies of Renfrew and Abbot Schaw, before the twelve Lords Auditors of Parliament that day,—Bishop Elphinston being president, and which I will specially notice again in the 4th chapter.

Abbey of Bangour, Ireland.

The Bangour referred to in the foregoing quotation from the Breviary, is situated in the County of Down, Ireland, and Saint Comhgall was both the founder and Abbot of the Abbey there. The annals of Ulster and Clonmacnoise record that Saint Comhgall was born in the year 510, and died in the year 600, at ninety years of age, and fiftieth year of his Abbotship. If the Breviary compiler is correct in the statement, although he could not give the date, that Mirinus was a pupil of Congallus, the other writers of the annals nearly fix the time of the sojourn of Mirinus to be in the end of the sixth and beginning of the seventh century.

Charter of Erection of Burgh of Paisley

In the charter of King James IV., sealed on 19th August, 1488, erecting the village of Paisley into a burgh, one of the chief causes assigned for the erection was "for the singular respect we have "for the glorious confessor, Saint Mirin." The charter also granted the power of holding two public fairs yearly forever,—"one on the day of "Saint Mirin, and the other on the day of Saint "Marnock." The fixing of Saint Mirin's fair on his festival day implies that the day was well known at that time, and that fair was accordingly held on 15th September until the fairs of Paisley were increased and the day altered. In confirmation of Saint Mirin being buried at Paisley, I may refer to the charter of Abbot George Schaw to the Provost, Bailies, Burgesses, and community of Paisley, dated 21st May, 1491, of the Common Hall or Town's House, at the market-place of Paisley, and the latter being taken bound to pay 19s. 8d. yearly "for the sustentation and repara-"tion of light to the altar of Saint Mirin and his "tomb there." On 15th July, 1499, James Crawfurd, of Kilwynnet, burgess of Paisley, and Elizabeth Galbraith, his wife, granted a charter of mortification, founding a chapel with a chaplain in the church of the Parish of Paisley, on the south side thereof, to the altar of Saints Mirin and Columba, and endowed it with the lands of Seidhill and Wellmeadow. On 3rd January, 1576, King James VI. granted a charter for erecting a Grammar School in Paisley, and endowed it with all the altarages, pittances of money, obit silver, and commons, formerly possessed and lifted by the monks of the Monastery of Paisley, and the first-named of these is the altar of Saints Mirin and Columba.

The only other chronicle I will refer to is the Black Book of Paisley,—not for anything contained in it, but because it has been called by that name. It is a transcript of the Scotichronicon of John Fordun, copied by John Gibson, jun., Canon of Glasgow and Rector of Renfrew, in the year 1501. Other monastic establishments made similar copies of Fordun, and they were generally called by the name of the monastery in which they were kept. The Paisley copy is now in the British Museum, and there is another copy in the Advocates' Library, Edinburgh.

Marginal notes:

Charter of the Common Hall.

Chapel of Saints Mirin and Columba.

Charter of Grammar School.

Black Book of Paisley.

William Forbes Skene's critical examination of legendary histories.

These legendary histories of Fordun and Elphinston have been critically examined by Mr. William Forbes Skene, of Edinburgh, who read an able paper on the subject in June, 1861, at the meeting of the Society of Antiquaries for Scotland, which was printed in their transactions, Vol. IV., p. 300, and reprinted in the Scotichronicon, or Catalogue of Scottish Bishops, by Rev. J. F. S. Gordon, D.D., Glasgow, page 70. Mr. Skene arrived at the conclusion that the tradition of Saint Regulus founding Saint Andrews in the fourth century cannot be relied upon, and that circumstances and events occurring in different centuries are mixed with fact and fable, and all so jumbled together, that these legendary stories are worthless. He is of opinion—and he seems to be correct—that Saint Andrews was founded in the eighth, and not in the fourth, century. With respect to Saint Mirin, there is a difference of 250 years between the Mirinus of Fordun and the Mirinus of Bishop Elphinston. The account of the latter Mirinus is a more plausible story than that of the former Mirinus, and it may be still incorrect. The Scotichronicon of 1386 may wholly, and the Aberdeen Breviary of 1484 may partially, be laid aside, leaving us to rely on the charter of endowment of the Monastery in 1165, followed by the Capitular seal, the charter of King James IV. in 1488, the charter of the Common Hall of Paisley in 1491, as contain-ing the only authentic history of Saint Mirin; and merely amounts to this, that Saint Mirin, the glorious confessor, lived and died, and an altar and a tomb was erected to his memory at Paisley; that the Church of Paisley was dedicated to him, and he was ejaculatorily addressed, "O Mirin!" and supplicated to "Pray to Christ for his servants;" that a small rivulet in Paisley was called by his sainted name, and a fair was ap-

Scotichronicon.

pointed to be held in Paisley on his festival day, the 15th of September.

There are several other places bearing the name of Mirin, which I will briefly notice.   1st. Inchmurrin, one of the islands in Loch Lomond.   The author of the Old Statistical Account of Scotland (1793, Vol. III., page 453) calls it *Inchmarin;* and the writer of the New Statistical Account (1845, Stirlingshire, page 90) calls it *Inchmurrin*, the island "of Saint Mirren, who was the tutelary "Saint of Paisley."   Irving, the historian of Dumbarton, also calls it Inchmurrin, and says it may have derived its name from Saint Mirren of Paisley.   The island of Inchmurrin, of all the islets in Loch Lomond, is nearest Balloch, and Balloch Castle was the early residence of the Lennox family until they removed to Inchmurrin. Balloch Fair is held on 15th of September, the festival of Saint Mirin; and the Fair has always been well frequented by people from Paisley. In support of that statement, I may refer to two of many cases,—(1) That of Robert Jardine, wright in Paisley, who died on 10th February, 1827, aged 73.   During the long term of 53 years, he regularly attended the Fair of Balloch, distant 15 miles from Paisley, without ever making a single omission.   (2) That of William Dunn of Barterholm, who died on 15th June, 1864, aged 93.   He attended the Fair for the long period of 71 years, whether the weather was foul or fair, his father before him having attended Balloch Fair most faithfully.   The Earls of Lennox, owners of Inch-Murrin, were great benefactors to the Monastery of Saint Mirin of Paisley. 2nd. Saint Mirron's Well, Kylsyth.   3rd. Kirkmirran, in the parish of Kelton, Kirkcudbrightshire.   It is stated both in the Old and New Statistical Account, that there was an ancient chapel and churchyard called Kirkmirran, now entirely neglected, and of which

Marginal notes:

Places bearing the name of Saint Mirin.

Balloch Fair.

nothing now is known but the locality and name. 4th. Knock Mirren, in the parish of Coylton, Ayrshire; and 5th, Burn of Mirran, in the parish of Edzel, Fifeshire.

After writing these observations respecting Saint Mirin, I would not be surprised to learn that the substance of the article in the *Aberdeen Breviary* had been contributed by Abbot George Schaw to Bishop Elphinston; that the narrative in the charter of King James IV. had been framed by Abbot Schaw; and that the obligation in the Charter of the Common Hall of Paisley had been written by Abbot Schaw. They read well in connection, and were all written within six years of each other. Abbot Schaw's attainments in learning and profound erudition secured for him the education of Prince James, Duke of Ross, second son of King James III. And King James IV. afterwards selected the Abbot for the office of High Treasurer of Scotland.

I may here state that the Right Reverend Alexander Penrose Forbes, D.C.L., Bishop of Brechin, has this day, 1st March, 1872, published a splendid work, called "Kalendars of Scottish Saints," and supplied a department sadly deficient in Scots literature. His book contains all the calendars of former compilers. In completing the Lives of the Saints he has bestowed great care, and furnished a complete system of Scots Hagiology, which will become the reference-book for the Saints of Scotland, from its excellent dictionary form and full index.

In the year 1505, Abbot Robert Schaw purchased from John Stewart, cook, burgess of Paisley, and Margaret Smith, his wife, a property on the east or opposite side of the vennel, extending therefrom to the road leading from the bridge to the market-place, called the

" Brigend," now forming part of High-street ; and
the Abbot was to give in exchange the tenement
called the Ladyhoill or Lady Houss, and also to
deliver to the cook and his wife half-a-chalder of
meal during the lifetime of Abbot George Schaw,
then a pensioner on the Monastery, and after his
decease, a whole chalder yearly out of the girnell
of the Monastery.   The contract was completed
by a charter written in Scots, the only one in that
language in the chartulary, of which the following
is a copy.

"CHARTER OF JOHN STEWART OF PROPERTY IN SAINT MIRIN'S WYND.

" Be it kend til al men be thyr prnt lres we Robert
be ye permissione of god Abbot of paslay and ye
universal convent of ye samyng with ane ful consent
and assent to be bindyin and oblyst and be thyr pre-
sents stratly binds and oblysis us and or Abbay and
successors til ane worthy man Jhone steward cuyk
burgess of or burgh of paslay That for sameikle as ye
said Jhone steward has analeit and sauld til us and or
abbay and Convent al and hail his tenement lying in
the said burgh of paslay with the pertinains betwix
or lands byggit be schir John mouss on ye west and
norcht pt and the lands of thomas ynglis on ye eist pt
and the he gait on the south pt And yropone has purely
and sympylly be staf and baston resignit in or hands
in convynit chaptor ye said tenement togidder with al
richt had be hym of the samyn wt the pertinents And
atour margret smyt spouse to the said John hass of her
fre wil and motiff noyr strenzeit nor compellit of the
qlk sche maid fath and ath apone a buyk outwith ye
prens of hir husband bot for hir awne profit and utility
has purily and sympylly ressyned gyffynd or hyr
coniuctfeftment of ye said tenement for eivar mar here-
fore we the said Robt abbot of paslay and convent of
the samyng or utilite and profyt promist and consentit
has gefand and grantit and be yr or lres gyffen and
grantit to the said John Steward and to margret
smyt his wif and to the langer lefar of ym twa

Charter to John
Stewart of the
Lady Houss.

Description.

conjunctly and severally al and hail or tenement
callit ye lady hoil or lady houss quhar now margret
wallass dwellis lyand in or burgh of paslay in sanct
Mirins wynd apone the west part of ye samyng betwix
ye lands of Marioun schelis on the west and norcht
pt and saint Mirins burne on the southt pt and the he
gait apone ye est pt with ye pertinains in liferent And
for al ye tyme termys and yeres of yr lyftyme and to
the langar lefar of ye said Johne steuard and margret
smyt his spouse alanarly And yt to be had and
possessyt be ye saids Jhone and Margit and to ye
longar lefar of yam twa in lyfrent quietly wel and in
peiss wtout ony maill or annuell or ony other exaction
to be payit til us or or abbay or ony oyr in or name
indurying ye lyffe of ye saids Jhone and margret
allanarly And als we ye saids Abbot and convent weil
alvisyt in or cheptor nowyit of conscience and of
cherite bynd us and oblysis us and or abbay and
successors lelyly and treuly be ye fathle and treuthly
upon or bodies to pay and causit be gefyn and
deliverit to ye said Jhone steward for his said tenement
forsaid and for his services done til us and or abbay
yerly at usit termys al and hail half ane chald of meil
of or girnell for al the tymes termys days and yeres of
ye lyfetyme of our venerabyll fader George schaw
pensionar off paslay And after ye deciss of ye said
venarabil fader. George pensionar of paslay the said
John steuard beand on lyfe and levand We the foresaid
Abbot and convent bynds and oblysis us or Abbay and
successors as off befor to pay geif and deliver yerly to
the said John steuard for all ye dais of his lyff
allanarly ane hail chaldr of meill out of or girnell of
paslay wt syklyk met and mesor as the said Jhone taks
nou and of befor And yis hail chaldr of meill to be
thankfully payit to the said Jhone steward and his
factors at his dymand eft ye decesst of ye said
venerabyll fader George pensionar of paslay indurying
lyf of the said Jhone allanarly and til nane oyris no
zit na oyr manner of way bot as said is And that yis
or prnt lres obligator and al ponts abone expremyt in
ye samyng be fermly and stabyll obstuit and frepit
We the said Robt be the permission of God Abbot of

*paslay and hail vniversal convent of ye samyng fermly
and straitly bynds and oblysis us lelyly and trewly be
ye fathtf and trewthf in or bonds and or abbay and
successors but fraud gyle or ony cavillatioun or
impediment to be proponit in the contrar qt soever And
for the mar strenth to yr or lres of obligatioun we haf
gart hyng to or convents siell of chapter At or abbay of
paslay ye* XXVI *day of ye monetht of Januar in the zer
of god a thousand fyf hundreth and fyf zers befor yr
witness Alan steward of ye Orchart James pantor
Schir dauid logane Donald lowfut thome lowre wt oyrs
divers.*"

Date.

This charter is a fine specimen of the Scots
language and orthography spoken and written in
Scotland 365 years ago, and not like the modern
Scotch orthography written at the present day,
as vulgar as possible.

The house referred to in the foregoing charter,
biggit by Sir John Mouss, was erected at the
north-east corner of Saint Mirin's-wynd in 1471,
and John Stewart's property lay around it to the
east and south. Sir John Mouss was appointed
Chamberlain of the Monastery, and the villagers
called the house the "Chamberlain's House." I
shall notice this property called the Chamberlain's
House again, from a sad calamity that happened
to that part of the town, commencing in a subsequent house built on the site of that property.

Chamberlain's
House.

I will now return to the Lady Houss, quhar
Margaret Wallas, a tenant of the convent, dwelt,
lyand apone the west part of the same. The
words, "Lady hoill," only appear in the charter
above quoted, and in subsequent titles of the
property it is called by the designative name of
the LADY HOUSS. The Lady Houss had perhaps,
by 1432, become considerably decayed and unfit
for the residence of the lady priest, and part of it
had been feued out by Abbot John Lithgow to
John de Schelis. It also appears, from the

Lady houss,
St. Mirin's wynd.

F

Sir John Wan.

description in the charter of John Stewart, that Marion Sheilis was the proprietrix of the upper portion of the Lady House tenement. She was probably either a daughter or grand-daughter of the first vassal, for the period between the dates of the two charters is seventy-three years. Sir John Wan was chaplain of the Lady Altar, when the dismemberment of the Lady House property in Saint Mirin's-wynd commenced. He erected another house in the royal highway, on what is now the site of the properties 14, 15, and 16 High-street. Sir John Wan's new house would then be the westmost building in the ancient ecclesiastical village of Paisley, which consisted of a few houses clustered near the bridge, and let by the Monastery at rents varying from 3s. to 13s. Scots yearly. Several houses or boothies were scattered along the road westward, on the lands of Priorscroft and Oxschawside, and also in Causeyside, occupied by the tenants of the Abbey, at the rent of 13s. Scots yearly, for an acre of land with a house or boothie on it. The tenement on the east side of the new Lady House was afterwards feued to Roland Muir, on the 12th June, 1490, and is described as bounded by the tenement formerly of Sir John Wan on the west; and the tenement on the east of the Lady House was also afterwards feued to Robert White, on 20th July, 1511, and is described as bounded by the tenement formerly of Sir John Wan on the east. In "The

Lady Altar.

"Rentall of all the Dewties that perteins zeirlie to "the haill altaris within the Paroche Kirk of "Paslay," given in the *Paisley Magazine*, p. 525, the first mentioned is OUR LADY ALTAR, and is entered as follows:—"Hes of propertie lyand "thereto, ane tenement of land, lyand on the "south side of the hie street, that anis was "heritabillie vmqll Sir Robert Wanis, he beand "Lady Priest, foundit it, and doted it to our

"Lady Altar for euir, as ane instrument, in Mr.
"Walter Stewards, prothogall buik beris, dated
"8th August, aᵒ 1511, now devydit into three tene-
"ments, ane occupeit be vmqll Wm. Alexander's
"wyiff, the second be Elizabeth burneheid, and
"the third be thomas petir." In the Rental of
the Pittances (*Paisley Magazine*, page 685) is the
following entry :—"Our Lady houss, occupeit of
"auld be our lady priest, and now be sundrie
"tenants." In the back wall of the staircase of
the house No. 14 High-street, erected in 1745,
now belonging to Mr. Alexander Macausland, boot
and shoe maker there, a carved stone, about a foot
square, has been built in for preservation ; and,
from the appearance of the sculpture, may either
have belonged to the Lady House in High-street,
or the previous Lady House in Saint Mirin's-
wynd, but most likely the former. The subject
seems to represent "Hospitality,"—a stranger
lying in a bed,—and expresses the language of
Job, "The stranger did not stay without : my
"door was open to the traveller," chap. xxxi.,
verse 32 ; and that of Saint Peter, "Using
"hospitality one towards another without mur-
"muring," 1 Peter, chap. iv., verse 9. That
sculptured stone, upwards of 450 years old, is one
of the few relics of ancient buildings in Paisley,
and might with great propriety be transferred to
the Free Public Museum, if the proprietors
were willing to grant it. The Wan family seem
to have been of an hospitable disposition, for
Martin Wan,—Vicar of Dreghorn in 1455, Dean of
the University of Glasgow in 1463, Almoner and
Confessor to King James III., and Chancellor to
the Metropolitan Church of Glasgow from 1470 to
1501,—on 1st June, 1501, mortified several sums
to Saint Nicholas Hospital in Glasgow, to provide
a bed for a poor and indigent person in the
hospital. Sir John (or Robert) Wan of Paisley,

Margin notes:

Lady houss, High-street.

Hospitality of the Wan family.

Martin Wan.

and Martin Wan of Glasgow, were perhaps related to each other either as brothers or uncle and nephew, and were both benevolent men. Sir John Wan, of Paisley, mortified his property to the altar of Our Lady, the blessed Virgin; and Martin Wan, of Glasgow, mortified several subjects for a chapel dedicated to Saint James. The stone that originally would be in the front of the house of Sir John Wan, represented a person lying on a bed, and Martin Wan granted a donation for a bed for an indigent person, the benevolence of both flowing in a similar direction.

I shall now return to Saint Mirin's-wynd. The longest liver of the two life-renters, John Stewart and Margaret Smyth, of the old Lady House, died about 1517; for, on the 3rd July of that year, Abbot Robert Schaw granted a new charter to James Wache, his heirs and assignees, of all and whole that tenement which is commonly called the "Lady House," lying in our Burgh of Paisley, in the south part thereof, near the burn of Saint Mirin,—containing, in the fore front, in the east, upon the common street, 25 ells of Burgall land, and so descending to the said burn of Saint Mirin; and in the front to the south, containing, on said burn, 23½ ells; and containing, on the south-west part of the garden of Robert Bysset and Elizabeth Landells, 27¾ ells of Burgall land; and so ascending and descending. There is a note or memorandum added at the end of this charter, stating that Robert Wache, the grandson of the former vassal, had assigned the property on 23rd November, 1546, to John Aitken. In 1539, a John Aitkyn, brewer in Paisley, was proprietor of a property in Causeyside; and in 1591, a John Atkin was proprietor of the property now No. 84 High-street, Paisley, on the east side of the old "West Port." On a stone tablet, which was in front of the house of the latter property, the paraphrase of the

Lady House, now James Wache.

The Aitken family.

1st verse of the 7th Psalm was inscribed in fine Saxon letters : —

```
O LORD MY GOD I PVT MY   TRA
AND CONFIDENCE IN THEE· | IST
SAVE ME FROM THAME THAT
                 ME PERSEW
AND EIK DELYVER ME
            IOHNE ATKIN A.D.1591
```

The stone now forms the lintel of the back-door of the present house, which was erected in 1783, and now belongs to Dr. Donald. In making these occasional digressions, I do it for the purpose of embracing as many of the interesting antiquities of the town as possible, with the view of preserving them.

The property conveyed by Abbot Lithgow to John Shields continued in that family upwards of a century, when a charter, dated 13th October, 1544, was granted, by Abbot John Hamilton, to Patrick Lowre, burgess of Paisley, of all and whole that tenement in the south part of the Burgh of Paisley, between the tenement formerly Andrew Ros, *alias* Payntor, on the west and north parts, containing at the head 9¼ ells, and descending along the tenement of Andrew Payntor and the common vennel, to the tenement of James Wesche,—containing, in the fore front, 35¼ ells ; along the lands of James Weshe to Saint Mirin's burn, 27 ells ; and ascending along the property of Andrew Payntor, 38¼ ells. The properties in this charter and that of James Wesche are very accurately described, notwithstanding the angular position of Saint Mirin's-wynd, Saint Mirin's burn, and Causeyside, and is as well expressed as it could be written at the present day. The charters already referred to are all the charters granted by the Abbots of Paisley that I can find concerning the property in Saint Mirin's-wynd called the Lady House, or west side of the street.

A gap generally occurs in the names of the pro-

Patrick Lowre's property.

Gap in the history of Paisley.

prietors of Paisley during the troublous times of
the Reformation and the forfeiture of Claud
Hamilton, commendator of the Abbey, and until
his being created Lord Paisley in 1587. The
vassals of the Abbey were not pressed for renewal
of their investitures till the year 1600 ; and the
chartulary of Lord Paisley and his successors, the
Earls of Abercorn, for 50 years, containing all the
charters of the Regality of Paisley, have been lost,
and it is only from a stray charter, which has been
preserved by some of the vassals, that a few of
the names of the proprietors in the Burgh can be
discovered,—each such charter generally yielding
three names,—the vassal's own name and those of
the two conterminous proprietors bounding his
feü. A starting point is, however, obtained from
the list of Feu-duties and Pittance Rentals delivered by Lord Cochran to the town of Paisley,
when he sold the superiority of the Burgh to
them on 3rd May, 1658. In the Pittance Rental,
under the head, "Ye Burngait," the following
four entries will be found, into which the Lady
House lands had by that time been subdivided :—

Pittance Rental.

"ane tenement at ye Burn Port occupeit
    by ye wyif and aires of vmqle Stene
    Cumming heritor yr of .... xiijs
"ane tenement next thereto, perteining
    to Sandie Mure.............................   xxid
"ye next houss yrto, perteining to Thomas
    Hart ....,......   xvijd
"ye houss above perteining to Robert
    Gillies...   xvd"

Ports of Paisley.

The list commences at the foot of the street at the
Burn Port. There were five ports in Paisley at
that time. One on the Bridge, called the "Brig
Port." The bridge was built previous to the
erection of the Burgh of Paisley in 1488; and one
of the arches fell in 1702, was rebuilt in 1703,
wholly taken down in 1782, and rebuilt that year,

which is the bridge now in use. Another port at 34 and 83 High-street, called the "West Port." Another at 14 Moss-street, called the "Moss-raw Port." Another at the head of School-wynd, called the "Barnyard Port." And the port at the foot of Saint Mirin's-wynd, called the "Burn Port," "South Port," and "Saint Mirin's Port." These, it may be said, embraced the town of Paisley, and the population in 1658 would be 1412. The burn at that period had to be forded from Saint Mirin's-wynd to Causeyside, and the roadway of the wynd was consequently very steep,—as steep as the Stoney-brae of the present day. I may also mention, that on the visitation of the Pest in January, 1600, when the population of Paisley would be 900, the Barnyard Port was ordered to be built up, the East and West Ports to be diligently watched, and the Burn Port and Moss-raw Ports to be simply closed,—the Burn Port was to be opened between 8 and 9 o'clock in the morning, and 4 and 5 in the afternoon.

The property mentioned in the Pittance Rental as belonging to the wife and heirs of the deceased Stephen Cumming, now Nos. 8 and 9 of Saint Mirin-street, was afterwards sold to Thomas Barr, in Gryfe Castle; afterwards inherited by his son, and sold by him to John Whyte, apothecary in Paisley. Sandie Muir's subjects, now Nos. 10 and 11 of the street, were acquired by William Greenlees, elder, cordoner, a bailie of Paisley; next, by William Greenlees, also a cordoner, and a bailie, and he disponed the east portion to his son William Greenlees, and the west portion to his son Robert Greenlees, afterwards a bailie. Thomas Hart's property, now No. 12 of the street, was afterwards acquired by James Adam, next by John Orr, then by James Robertson, and sold by him in 1669 to John Knox in Arcleston, and is described as situated in that vennell called Burn-

Properties Nos. 8 and 9 Saint Mirin-street.

gait. In 1677, John Knox sold the property to William, first Earl of Dundonald, Lord Cochrane of Paslaye and Ochiltree, at which time Knox was one of his Lordship's servants. His Lordship sold that property the same year, along with the property in High-street, erected by Andrew, Master of Sempill, in 1580 (taken down in 1862), to John Snodgrass, maltman in Paisley, afterwards elected a bailie in 1680, 1681, and 1682. He was succeeded by his son, Hew Snodgrass, writer in Paisley, who was chosen Town-Clerk of the Burgh in 1683. The late Campbell Snodgrass of Thornhill, a lineal descendant, who died on 7th February, 1851, was buried in the Paisley Cemetery. His relatives erected to his memory a handsome monument of the finest Italian white marble, in the Grecian style of architecture, sculptured with tasteful wreaths, and, standing in lofty grandeur on the highest part of the grounds, it has been for the last twenty years admired as the grandest monument in the whole Cemetery. On the west side is engraved the following inscription:—

Hew Snodgrass, Town-clerk.

" In Memory of
Hew Snodgrass Town clerk of Paisley 1639 "

There must be a mistake in the tradition of the family of that date, for Hew Snodgrass, with consent of his wife, Elizabeth Semple, conveyed the property to William Wallace, younger, maltman in Paisley, on 14th January, 1698. Robert Gillies's subject, now No. 13 of the street, descended to his son, Allan Gillies, and next to his brother, William Gillies, at Castlesemple. The latter sold the property in 1629, to Robert Mylner, in Castlesemple, and he was succeeded by his son, Robert Mylner, in 1637. He sold the property in 1642 to Walter Cochran, mason in Paisley, and he was succeeded by his son, Walter Cochran, cordoner,

burgess of Paisley, and he again, in 1674, sold it
to William Wallace, elder, maltman in Paisley.
The latter, on 4th January, 1698, disponed the
property to his son, William Wallace, younger.
It is described as "lying in that Vennell called
Burngait or St. Mirrines-wynd," and bounded by
the tenement of the deceased Claud Hamilton on
the west. In the Poll Tax Rolls for 1695, page
54, is the following entry :—"William Wallace,
"maltman, worth 500, and not 5000, mks 2 lib
"16 sh ; Agnes Ferguson, spouse, 6 sh ; William,
"Agnes, and Elizabeth Wallace, children, each
"6 sh ; Helen Temple, servant, 12 lib fie 12 sh."
In the chancel of Paisley Monastery there is a
tombstone with the following inscription :—"In
"memory of William Wallace, who died 1716, in
"the 88th year of his age, and Agnes Ferguson, his
"spouse, and William Wallace, their son, who died
"in 1745, in the 76th year of his age, and Janet
"Kibble, his spouse, and is the burying place of
"James Wallace, their son, and Jean Miller, his
"spouse, and their family, 1779." William Wallace, younger, will appear again in the chapter on
the *Unhouss.* I have now brought the proprietors
down to the end of the 17th century.

In the beginning of the 18th century, the houses
in Saint Mirin's-wynd were principally composed
of timber in the front, the roofs thatched with
straw, bent, or heather, and the ridges covered
with turves. Those houses that were raised two
storeys high had their stairs leading directly from
the narrow wynd. The houses generally belonged to,
or were tenanted by, cordoners, who tanned their
own leather. The only house which was slated
was situated at the north-east corner of the street,
erected on the site of the Chamberlain's house,
biggit by Sir John Mouss in 1471. Robert, Master
of Sempill, Bailie of the Regality of Paisley
(afterwards Robert the third and great Lord Sem-

Marginal notes: Timber houses. / Chamberlain's house.

G

Belltrees family.

pill), acquired the Chamberlain's house in 1548 from Abbot Hamilton, which he afterwards granted to his youngest son, John Sempill of Belltrees, vulgarly called the "Dancer," who married Mary Livingston, one of the four Marys of Queen Mary. His eldest son, Master James Sempill, was educated along with the young King James VI., and John, Lord-Erskine, son of the Earl of Mar (afterwards Regent), under the learned George Buchanan. James Sempill succeeded his father in 1579, and the King afterwards knighted his schoolfellow. Robert, fourth Lord Sempill, Sheriff Principal of Renfrew Sheriffdom, and Bailie of the Regality of Paisley, on 17th February, 1602, appointed Sir James Sempill of Belltrees Sheriff Depute and Bailie Depute ; and on 9th March following Sir James took the oath of office in presence of the Right Honourable James, Master of Paisley, Provost of the Burgh, and Thomas Inglis and Robert Algie, the Bailies thereof. In the Pittance Rental of Paisley this property is entered as follows :—

Heigh houssis.

"The heyt houssis and tenements now at ye
"Croce perteining to Sir James Sempill of bill-
"tries knight, wes of auld ij tenements, qrof the
"heyt houss was callit ye Challmerlainis houss,
"and payit yeirlye ———, and the vither
"tenement, qr the hall is now, wes anis vmqle
"Martha Hamiltones and payit yeirlie of pit-
"tancis ———zeit therefter coft all yaim viz
"25 Maij anno 1548 be Robert Master of Sym-
"pill yan payand yeirlie vilib iijs iiji yan."

Author of Habbie Simson.

Sir James Sempill conveyed the property to his eldest son, Robert Sempill, who succeeded in 1625. Robert Sempill was the author of the elegy on Habbie Simson, the piper of Kilbarchan. He conveyed the property, in 1653, to John Fork, writer in Paisley, son of Robert Fork, Sheriff-Clerk of Renfrewshire. John Fork was elected

Town-Clerk of Paisley on 3rd October, 1678, and he conveyed the property to John Campbell, apothecary in Paisley; who was succeeded by his eldest son, Robert Campbell, surgeon. The shoone (shoe) market was held in front of this property to the bridge, and the clothes market was held in front of the houses at the Cross, where the Coffee-Room is now situated.

In the beginning of the year 1711, St. Mirin's Port was removed, and the burn flagged. The flagging of the burn and raising of the roadway of Saint Mirin's-wynd was considered a vast improvement in connecting that road with Causeyside, and raising them both considerably higher at that low part. In 1712, the inhabitants of the district petitioned the Council to remove the holding of the fairs from St. James's acre, at the foot of Wangate-end (Moss-street), to the south Port *alias* Saint Mirin's Port. The Council, on considering the application, appointed the Beltan fair of that year to be held there.

Removal of Saint Mirin's Port.

This now brings me down to 1733, when one of the greatest calamities occurred in Saint Mirin's-street that ever happened to the town of Paisley. William Semple, thus noticing it in his history of Paisley, printed in 1782, says,—"In June, " 1733, this town suffered greatly by fire. The " conflagration was kindled in Mr. Campbell " the then surgeon's shop, head of Saint Mirran's- " wynd, and wholly consumed the said wynd, " with part of the Causeyside adjacent thereto, " and part of the south side and east of the main " street, with part of the north side of the area " of the Cross, became a prey to the violence of " the flames." I wish to add a few more particulars to that account of this destructive fire. On Saturday, 2nd June, 1733, a fire happened in the laboratory of Robert Campbell, doctor of physic, at the head of the shoe market, between

Great Fire in 1733.

four and five o'clock in the afternoon, and being a fine dry summer afternoon, the sparks thrown out by the flames at once kindled the inflammable materials of the adjoining houses, which spread with fearful rapidity from house to house, east, south, west, and north, and by the following Sabbath morning 31 houses were burned to the ground, 80 families rendered houseless, and 400 out of the small population of 3396, made homeless. It was a heartrending scene, and the inhabitants were nearly paralysed by the appalling conflagration. The flames flew down the houses on the east side of the wynd, set those on fire on the west side, spreading south and north, and westward at the Cross to the property No. 10 High-street. The devouring element was at the same time devastating the houses to the bridge, crossed the street in a similar manner as in the wynd, proceeding northwards by the narrow passage, vulgarly called the "Hole o' the wa'," to the Dyers'-wynd, crossed the passage, and burned the house that formerly stood on the site of Gilmour-street. That was the second great fire in Paisley in the course of four years. The other one happened in Causeyside, when 30 families were burned out of house and home. The loss of property was considerable, from several of the houses being situated in a wealthy part of the town, and the distress of the sufferers very great. A meeting of the Presbytery having taken place on the 20th of June following, the Bailies presented a petition and representation in behalf of the sufferers by the late terrible conflagration. The Presbytery heard the petition, thought it most reasonable, granted its desire, and appointed a voluntary contribution to be made from house to house in all the parishes within the bounds of the Presbytery, betwixt and the next meeting. That next meeting was held at the Mearns Kirk on

25th July following, for the ordination of George M'Vey, when the following collections, in sterling money, for the sufferers by the late fire at Paisley, were handed in :—

Collections for the sufferers.

Eastwood,	£12 18 0
Erskine,	8 0 0
Greenock,	15 0 0
Houston,	1 5 0
Inchinnan,	3 6 8
Innerkip,	6 10 0
Kilbarchan,	20 0 0
Killellan,	5 11 11
Kilmalcolm,	7 5 0
Lochwinnoch,	7 5 6
Paisley,	61 1 8½
Port-Glasgow,	12 13 2
Renfrew,	20 0 0

£180 16 11½

The parishes of Mearns and Neilston are not mentioned as contributors to the fund.*

The Town Council, on 13th July, 1733, held a meeting and took into consideration the great losses this Burgh had been suffering of late by fire, one of which had happened within these four

Prohibiting the erection of timber houses.

---

* The late William Ferrier, D.D., minister of the Associate Congregation, Oakshaw-street, Paisley, preached a sermon in the High Church of Paisley, on July 1, 1798, to the friends of the Sabbath schools, afterwards printed by Neilson & Weir. The Doctor, to stimulate his hearers to liberality, referred to the contributions for the sufferers by the fire, and addressing his auditors as inhabitants of Paisley, said (at page 153),—" Of late you had occasion repeatedly to manifest " your zeal to relieve suffering humanity. Still, you supported " your character ; and what the fires had consumed your " liberality promptly restored." There is a note added, explaining that the Doctor's remarks had reference to some very liberal contributions which had been made in Paisley on two occasions, for the benefit of a multitude of persons whose houses and effects had been destroyed by fire; and in the first of those cases the distribution of the fund was superintended by the gentlemen who were in the Magistracy.

years in Calsasyde, whereby a great many houses were consumed, and particularly the other that broke out on the second of June last, at the head of the shoe mercat, whereby eighty families were burned out of their houses. The Council also considering that the streets of the Burgh are very strait and narrow in many places, which cannot easily be made wider and broader, and that a great many houses fronting to the streets are thatched with straw and heather, and some of them built with timber fronts, which are ready fuel to the fire in such conflagrations, so that when such accidents have happened, all means used for preventing the spreading thereof have proved ineffectual. The Council then enacted and ordained, That no person build houses fronting to the street in time coming, within the ports of the Burgh, or the places where the ports were, but such as shall be built with stone walls, both back and fore, and covered on the roof with slate, tile, lead, or stone : And that all houses which were ruinous, or should thenceforth become ruinous, be built and covered in manner foresaid : And that all houses of two storeys fronting to the street thereafter to be built or repaired without the ports, should in like manner be built of stone and covered with sclate, tyle, lead, or stone.

New buildings erected.

Several of the lairds of the burned houses were ruined by the conflagrations, and were under the necessity of disposing of their steadings, and others experienced considerable difficulties in rebuilding. All the houses in the burned district have been erected since 1733, and some of these have since been taken down and replaced by handsome buildings. Those that remain on both sides of Saint Mirin's-street are ripe for removal; not only for rebuilding, but for the widening of the street. The houses rebuilt between St. Mirin's-wynd and the Bridge, then called the "Brigend," were

built in the "Nepus" style of architecture,—a
style very prevalent in the extension of the
town in 1780. *Cnaep* (Saxon), a top or summit;
hus (Saxon), a house,—Nepus, a house on the top
of a house. These houses have been supplanted
by handsome buildings. The four houses from
St. Mirin's-street to No. 10 High-street, and the
house on the site of Gilmour-street, at the "Hole
o' the wa'," of three and four storeys high, were
built in the Flemish style of architecture, and
with twin craw-stepped gables to the front,—a
style which gave the cross of Paisley a very
ancient-looking appearance. The half of one of
these houses that still remains will form part of
the subject of Chapter IV. of this article. The
houses erected in the wynd were of a more humble
character of two storeys, and would be considered good dwellings in their day.

The element of fire, according to the old adage,
is a good servant, but a bad master. When it
assumes the latter character among old houses, it
is the best renovator that can visit an ancient
town. In the present instance, it reduced to
ruins a district covered with erections of inflammable material, very dangerous to a community, by
keeping them continually in terror and alarm for
fire, and causing an edict to be issued commanding the walls of all houses built in future, to be
composed of stone and not of timber.

Fire the best renovator of an old town.

The excellent rules laid down by the Town
Council, that all houses fronting the street should
be built with stone walls, and the roofs covered
with slate, tile, lead, or stone, have been observed
regarding the walls; but the covering of roofs
with the material ordered were the exceptions,
thatching with straw continuing the rule of the
builders. One of the houses in the wynd, seen
from the Cross or market-place, is covered with
thatch at the present day.

Evasion of building rules.

A writer in the "Scots Magazine," in 1786, page 619, respecting Paisley in 1733, says—"The "houses are mean in their appearance, the streets "narrow and dirty, and the people slovenly in "their dress and manners;" while, in 1786, "The houses are mostly new and elegant, the "streets spacious and well paved, the people gay "and polite, and the servant-maids more neatly "dressed, with their caps, gauzes, and white "stockings, than were formerly the citizens' "wives."

The properties have now become more sub-divided; and I think the proper course to follow is to take them up separately, commencing at the foot of Saint Mirin-street and going upwards, according to the rental of the town in 1658, and the street numbers of the present day. I will therefore begin with No. 8, now the property possessed by the Bank of Scotland.

I have already stated that it belonged to John White, and his name will be found in the Poll Rolls, page 59, "John Whyte, apothecarie,

"12 lib 6 sh, Robert John and Agnes Whytes his "children, each 6 sh, Jean Young sert 2 lib fee, "1s and 6 sh general pole, £13 17s. 6d." That entry shows the doctor was occupying a respectable position in society. He was related to the Bargarran family, and attended Christian Shaw, the girl who pretended to be bewitched. His brother-in-law, Doctor John Johnston, also attended her. Dr. Whyte, before his death, executed bonds of provision in favour of his three children, John, Helen, and Christian Whytes, to the amount of 3000 merks scots. Robert Whyte, his eldest son, being unable to liquidate these bonds, the younger children in 1720 obtained an adjudication against him and the property. John Whyte, younger, had become a writer in Edinburgh, and afterwards a Depute Clerk in the

Court of Session. Mr. John Whyte was in the habit of visiting Paisley occasionally, and at the end of 1745 he happened to be there on one of these visits. A rumour reached Paisley on Saturday, 28th December, that Prince Charles, the Pretender's son, had levied clothing from the citizen burgesses of Glasgow, for his motley and ragged regiment of Highland soldiers, and that he would soon be in Paisley. The Bailies called a hurried meeting of the Town Council that Saturday evening, to make preparation for any emergency, in case of a similar levy being made on the weaver town. The meeting was held, and appointed Mr. John Whyte, one of the Depute Clerks of Session (who happened to be in the place at the time); Mr. Rob. Campbell, doctor of medicine in Paisley; William Caldwell, William Reid, late Bailies; Mr. John Baird and Robert Pollock, merchants,—a committee to treat with the pretended Government of Prince Charles, the Council becoming bound to ratify any agreement that might be made by the committee. On the Sunday afternoon following, an officer, with 150 of the rebel army, passed through Paisley, on a marauding excursion to Blackston, the residence of Alexander Napier, a commander of a militia regiment that had harassed the rebels considerably. In passing through Paisley, one of the officers left a letter at Bailie Fulton's house in Causeyside, which turned out to be a military summons, commanding Bailie Kyle, Bailie Storie, and William Park, merchant in Townhead, to appear in the Secretary's office, at twelve o'clock noon, on Monday, under pain of military execution against their goods and persons. A meeting of the Bailies, Council, and inhabitants was held that Sunday evening, when it was agreed that Bailie Kyle; William Park; John White, depute clerk; William Cald-

Margin notes:
Rebellion of 1745.

Raid to Blackston.

H

Prince Charles fining Paisley.

well, merchant, Causeyside; and John Robertson, weaver, there; should form the deputation to meet with the Prince and his secretary, John Murray of Broughton, writer to the signet, Edinburgh. The deputation attended on the Monday, and a fine of £1000 was demanded from them. The deputation explained the poverty of the town, and the few inhabitants in the place; the population then being only 3913. Bailie Kyle and Mr. Park were detained as hostages till the fine was paid. Mr. Whyte, who would know the Prince's secretary, Murray, called on Tuesday, the 31st January, 1745, and had a conversation with Mr. John Hay, writer to the signet, Edinburgh, another of the Prince's attendants, regarding a mitigation of the fine, when the latter stated that the Prince had agreed to accept £500,—a sum which, after considerable difficulty, was raised and paid to Andrew Lumsden, clerk to the secretary, another Edinburgh writer. It would therefore appear that the army of the young Adventurer was composed of hungry, ill-clad Highlanders, and his Court filled with needy Edinburgh lawyers,—two classes of society totally unable to cope with a disciplined army and British statesmen.

John Renfrew, smith.

John Renfrew, smith, in Paisley, in 1733, obtained an assignation to Whyte's decreet of adjudication and debt. He had previously, in 1732, acquired right to the southmost half of the lands of Blackhole, which will be noticed in Chapter II. of this article. His son, John Renfrew, was served heir in 1747, and he obtained a charter of adjudication from the Town Council of Paisley, of these two tenements in the vennel called Burngate. The latter syllable, *gate*, is generally spelled *gait*, and is not derived from the fact of a port having at one time been situated at the burn, but from the Saxon word *gait*, a street,—Burngait,

Burn-street. John Renfrew, the son, was a merchant in Paisley in 1747, afterwards resided in Gallowhill, and in 1756 at Hillhead, and again a merchant in Paisley in 1780. John Renfrew was appointed an ensign in the militia company raised in Paisley against the Pretender's son, Prince Charles. The company was inspected by the Earl of Home and staff, on Saturday, 1st December, 1745, and the following Sabbath-day they marched to Glasgow for Stirling, to the martial music of the drum and fife, the colours of the company being carried by Ensign Renfrew —better known by the name of "Gentle John." He was present at the battle of Falkirk, fought on Friday, 17th January, 1746, when eight men belonging to the Paisley company were killed. That ensign or colours afterwards did duty as a flag on Kings' birthdays, at the Municipal Buildings at the market-place of Paisley, till 1821, and afterwards on the turrets of the County Buildings till Saturday, 24th May, 1856, when the last shred of it, fluttering in the breeze, was blown away.

John Renfrew, in 1780, disponed the subjects to John Renfrew, weaver in Paisley, his eldest son. In the Paisley department of the *Glasgow Directory* for 1783, he is entered John Renfrew, manufacturer, Causeyside. John Renfrew afterwards became a bleacher at Cochranfield, near Johnstone, and in 1797 he sold the subjects to John Ralston, changekeeper in Paisley. A "changekeeper" was a small innkeeper, and "Ralston's" was very much frequented. The changekeeper died in 1805, and his widow carried on his business, and is entered in the *Paisley Directory* for 1810,—Mrs. Ralston, vintner, Saint Mirren's-street. Gavin Ralston, residing in Paisley, succeeded his father in 1805; and he, dying in 1814, was succeeded by his sister, Margaret

Ensign Renfrew.

Battle of Falkirk.

John Ralston, changekeeper.

Malcom Lang, dyer.

Ralston, who married Malcom Lang, dyer, Paisley. She died in 1818, having left the subjects to her husband in liferent, and Mr. Gavin Lang, writer in Paisley, his brother, in fee.

Malcom Lang carried on business in Dyers'-wynd for many years, in the work which was erected by his great-grandfather, John King, dyer, in 1738. His grandfather, William King, also carried on business in the same place, and he was elected a Bailie in 1764, '66, and '68. Malcom Lang's father, John Lang, was a dyer in Crawford's-dyke, near Port-Glasgow. The work in the Dyers'-wynd is the oldest dyework in Paisley, and now belongs to, and is occupied by, Walter Hogg, dyer. The wynd was previously called Litsters'-wynd, thereby implying that dyers had carried on business there. The word "litster" finds its origin in the dyeing lichen—*lit;* and that moss, with a little homely chemistry, could be made to produce various colours for dyeing wool.

Gavin Lang, writer.

Gavin Lang, writer in Paisley, the fiar of the subjects, was admitted a Procurator in Paisley, in November, 1802, and was elected treasurer of the Faculty of Procurators when their Royal Charter of Incorporation was obtained on 30th January, 1803. He continued treasurer for the long period of 35 years, and resigned on 2nd November, 1838. The Faculty agreed to present Mr. Lang with a testimonial, consisting of a silver coffee-pot and stand, and silver waiter, and on 22nd January, 1839, the presentation was made. The following inscription was engraved on the silver articles :—

Testimonial.

"Presented to Gavin Lang, esquire, by the Faculty of Procurators in Paisley, as an additional Testimonial of their appreciation of his very valuable and gratuitous services, as Treasurer to the Faculty, from the date of the Faculty Incorporation, in 1803, till his resignation in November, 1838."

Mr. Lang was elected Town-Clerk of Paisley on

17th July, 1827, and continued in that office till his death, on 30th January, 1845. Mr. Gavin Lang took an interest in archæological pursuits, and he collected a great number of official and judicial papers concerning witchcraft and the witches of Renfrewshire; and I recollect of handing him a few similar documents, to make his collection as complete as possible. After his death, I made inquiries concerning the whole collection; but I was informed they had never been seen. Mr. Lang, during his official career of Town-Clerk, copied the oldest minute books of the Town Council, commencing in 1594. These old books are written in old Saxon character, and some of the minutes were in a very cramp hand, and exceedingly difficult to decipher. The copies extended to two folio volumes in readable writing, and he presented them to the Town Council. They are indeed a monument of industry and perseverance, and might be printed periodically in one of the newspapers, in the same manner as those of the Town Council of Glasgow were given to the public several years ago. At the time Mr. Lang was poring over the venerable volumes of the Council proceedings, a message came to me to come and see him. On entering his apartment, Mr. Lang at once addressed me,—" I have found out Habbie Simson," seemingly as proud of the discovery as when the Syracusan geometrician, Archimedes, used the exclamation of a similar word, " Ἑύρηκα ! " —" I have found it." He showed me the entry about Robert Simson, piper, being put in the stocks for misbehaviour, with an old mark at the place, on which was written, in old writing, the words "Habbie Simson."

On 23rd September, 1833, The Body Corporate and Politic, constituted by Act of Parliament by the name of the Governor and Company of the Bank of Scotland, acquired the property. The

Marginal notes:

Archæological pursuits.

Habbie Simson, piper.

Bank of Scotland.

Bank, in the year 1835, erected the present pile of buildings thereon for their agency in this town, and it stands at the foot of St. Mirren's-street and Causeyside, resembling Ailsa Craig or the Bass Rock, a clumsy piece of architecture, blocking-up both streets; and the earlier the misshapen building is removed the better. The Bank of Scotland is the oldest establishment of the kind in the kingdom, having been instituted in 1695, by an Act of the Scots Parliament. James Findlay, manufacturer, Glasgow, son of John Findlay, D.D., of the High Church, Paisley, was appointed agent, and he opened the business of the Bank in the new premises on 8th March, 1836. At the date of erection, it was considered a good site between the Cross and Causeyside. Other Banks have since that time been drawn into the important thoroughfare to the railways, and the Bank of Scotland will probably be attracted in the same direction in a short time. Mr. Findlay died on the 22nd August, 1850, in the 66th year of his age. John Hutchison, the present agent, succeeded him.

No. 9 Saint Mirin-street.

The property No. 9 also belonged to John White, apothecary, and was sold by John Renfrew, smith, by public roup, on 27th August, 1733, and was purchased by Robert Fulton, merchant, commonly called Bailie Fulton. In September following, the Bailie executed an assignation in favour of Ludovick Stewart, carrier in Paisley, on the narrative that the house had been "made ruinous by the fire which happened in the Burgh on the second day of June last," and had purchased it for behoof of Ludovick Stewart. Ludovick accordingly built a house upon the site, but never paid the price; and John Renfrew partly interfered with the rents, as did, after his death, his son, John Renfrew. Ludovick died in 1734, and was succeeded by his son, Ludovick

Ludovick Stewart.

Stewart, a soldier, afterwards weaver in Paisley, who, in 1780, raised an action of count and reckoning against John Renfrew, and they came to an arrangement in September, 1780. In 1786, the Town Council raised and obtained decreet of declarator of non-entry against Ludovick Stewart, and took possession of the property. During the period from 1733 to 1786, the Stewarts had not obtained a conveyance from the Renfrews, and the former could not be received as vassals. The Town Council being in possession of the subjects, Ludovick Stewart entered into an arrangement with them about the non-entry duties and expenses, and obtained a conveyance from them in the latter year, to "All and Haill that house in "Water-wynd of Paisley, high and laigh, back "and fore, bounded by John Renfrew's house on "the south, by the Water-wynd on the east, and "William Montgomerie's house on the north." In 1798, Ludovick Stewart conveyed a portion of the property to his eldest son, Charles Stewart, soldier in the 23rd regiment of light dragoons; another portion to Ann Stewart, daughter, spouse of Kennedy Reid, shoemaker in Paisley; and another portion to his youngest son, William Stewart, shoemaker in Paisley. The name of "William Stewart, shoemaker, Saint Mirren's-street," will be found entered in the directory for 1810. In 1824, Charles Stewart conveyed his portion to Wilson Craig, hairdresser in Paisley, and his name is also entered in the same directory for 1810. The property now belongs to his trustees. Mrs. Reid and William Stewart's portions of the property were both acquired by Archibald Sinclair, hatter in Paisley, in 1818, and now belong to his trustees. Mr. Sinclair commenced business in High-street in 1812, in the east shop of the property built in 1580 by Andrew, Master of Sempill (which was taken down

Stewart family.

Wilson Craig.

Archibald Sinclair.

in 1862); and Mr. Sinclair continued in the old house for the long period of 40 years, and died in 1862, at the advanced age of 80 years. Mr. Sinclair's back shop, where he dressed hats, was very much frequented by the middle-class society, the shopkeepers in High-street, and occasionally a sprinkling of the aristocracy; and was called the "Goose Club," in honour of the chief implement used by Mr. Sinclair for pressing hats. Any person desirous of hearing both foreign and local news, but more particularly the latter, generally hied to Sinclair's back shop, *alias* the "Goose Club" room; and these individuals, on hearing the news of the day, the chit-chat of the hour, generally retired, leaving more gossip to be retailed by the parties left to the new comers. The club was a dry one, and the members could both take and give a joke, and were never seen to stagger when they left the club-room. The "Goose Club" was an institution of Paisley for several years, and Mr. Sinclair outlived many of its members; and I have merely noticed the circumstance, that it might be known that a club existed and flourished nearly half-a-century ago, without meeting in a house having above its door the words—tavern, vintner, or licensed to sell *spirits.*

William Greenlees, shoemaker in Paisley, was owner of the next property, now number ten of the street. He was one of the founders of the Cordoners' Society, on 16th December, 1703, and he signed the Charter of Incorporation by a mark. He was elected deacon of the trade in 1710, 1718, 1723, and 1731. In 1731, he was a widower, with two daughters, and he entered into a marriage with Janet Wilson, relict of John Paton, barber in Paisley, on 16th September, 1731, and she had two sons. He conveyed the property to her in liferent, and bound himself to maintain her youngest son, who was then ten years of age, until

Margin notes:

Goose Club.

No. 10 Saint Mirin-street.

William Greenlees.

he was sixteen, and she reserved her *jus relictæ*, derived from her former husband, for her own disposal. Neither of the contracting parties could write, and the contract of marriage was signed by Charles Simson and William Tarbat, notaries. On 14th April, 1742, she exercised her reserved right (no children having been born of the marriage) in favour of her sons, William Paton, then a barber, and Alexander Paton, then a shoemaker. She died shortly thereafter, and her two sons commenced a prosecution before the Sheriff of Renfrewshire, in the month of June following, against their stepfather. Alexander claimed 18 lib. Scots yearly for clothing for four years; and the two pursuers claimed the goods and gear reserved by their mother, and those that belonged to them as executors of their father, or £8 stg. which had been paid to him by the Magistrates of Paisley, for the effects belonging to their father, "in con-"sideration of the great loss sustained by the "fires consuming and destroying these," and which sum had been paid in addition to the sum of £50 stg. he received from the Magistrates on account of the burning of his house. Answers, replies, and duplies were lodged, and Sheriff-Substitute, Henry Maxwell, on 8th July, 1742, allowed parties a proof, the defender having denied liability. The pursuers lodged a reclaiming petition, and the Sheriff, on 9th August following, adhered, and the pursuers then abandoned their case. These circumstances again bring out the destructive character of the fire which happened in the year 1733, and the amount paid to one of the sufferers. It also gives a sample of litigations which frequently occur, when a widower and widow, both with families, contract second marriages. The property was next acquired by William Montgomery, mealman in Paisley, on 1st August, 1757. He was succeeded

Litigation between stepsons and a stepfather.

I

by his grandson, William Campbell, weaver in Paisley, son of Jean Montgomery, relict of Alex. Campbell, flesher in Paisley, afterwards spouse of John Anderson, manufacturer, and obtained a Precept of Clare Constat on 26th April, 1822. William Campbell, afterwards manufacturer in Glasgow, disponed the property to himself; John Anderson, weaver in Paisley; Jean Anderson, spouse of William Laird, hairdresser in Paisley; and Elizabeth Aitken, daughter of George Aitken, spouse of John Clark, thread-maker, Paisley.

No. 11 Saint Mirin-street.

Robert Greenlees.

The next property (now No. 11 of the street) was conveyed by Robert Greenlees, elder cordoner in Paisley, to Robert Greenlees, his son. Robert Greenlees was also a founder of the Shoemakers' Society, and was elected Deacon in 1711 and 1725, also a Bailie in 1720 and 1721. He sold the subjects to William Greenlees, his brother, who sold them to Alexander Campbell, shoemaker in Paisley, in 1754, and he was succeeded by his son, William Campbell, shoemaker in Paisley, in 1769.

Nos. 12 and 13 Saint Mirin-street.

William Wallace, maltman.

The next properties, Nos. 12 and 13 of the street, belonged to William Wallace, younger, maltman, then of Caversbank. In 1733 and 1745, he executed deeds of settlement in favour of his second son, James Wallace, maltman in Paisley (his eldest son, William, having predeceased), directing him to convey certain properties to his female grandchildren. The old man must have died between 4th and 16th of March, 1745. James Wallace, accordingly, on 31st May, 1746, conveyed the subjects to his two nieces, Margaret and Elizabeth Wallace, children of his deceased brother William. Mary Wallace, afterwards wife of John Gray, baker in Greenock, with his consent, and Elizabeth Wallace, with consent of Mary Rowan, her mother, and John Rowan, merchant in Glasgow, her uncle, her curators, conveyed the subjects (No. 12 in the street) to John Lillie, weaver in Paisley, on 14th and 21st May, 1748. He conveyed the property to William M'Alpine, taylor in Paisley, in 1758, who arrived twice at the dignity of Deacon of the Taylors' Society, in 1752 and 1761. He sold the subjects to William Campbell, shoemaker in Paisley, in 1770, who was appointed four times Deacon of the Incorporation of Shoemakers. The two properties (11 and 12) now belonged to one individual, and he and his brother commenced the business of tanners, and their names will be found in the Paisley department of the *Glasgow Directory* for 1783, — "William and Thomas Campbell, tanners, St. Marion's Wynd." The name of "Saint Mirin" has undergone many mutations since he came from Ireland in the 7th century, and this last one, "Marion," makes *him* an English woman. William Campbell executed a deed of settlement, conveying all his property to his brother, Thomas Campbell. Like his brother William, he was also appointed four times Deacon of the Shoemakers. Thomas Campbell, who died in April, 1810, by his deed of settlement, dated 1806, left the properties to his surviving sons, William Campbell, tanner, James Campbell, writer, and Edward Campbell, bleacher. On the death of William Campbell, tanner, on 31st October, 1817, his brothers succeeded to his share. Both brothers respectively conveyed their share to Elizabeth, Margaret, and Janet Campbell, in 1823 and 1826. The former died 3rd September, 1830, and the latter on 24th November, 1837. In 1849, Thomas Campbell, messenger-at-arms in Paisley, a grandson of Thomas Campbell, tanner, acquired the subjects, and he sold them in 1855 to Mrs. Mary Miller or M'Donald, wife of David M'Donald, sewed muslin manufacturer, Glasgow.

The subjects No. 13 of the street were con-

St. Marion's Wynd.

No. 13 Saint Mirin-street.

veyed in 1747, by Mary and Elizabeth Wallace,
with consent of their curators, to William Hercules, shoemaker in Paisley. He was Deacon of
the Shoemakers' Society in 1738. He was succeeded by his son, William Hercules, weaver in
Paisley, in 1763, and the same year he sold the
property to Walter M'Farlane, weaver in Paisley.
In 1782, Walter M'Farlane, with consent of his
wife, sold the property to Matthew Anderson,
mason in Glanderston; Matthew Anderson, to
John Rodger, farmer in Glanderston, 1789; John
Rodger, to Andrew Rodger, farmer in Tappitfauld,
1809; and John Rodger, farmer in Glanderston,
succeeded his father in 1846. John Rodger conveyed to John M'Arthur, manufacturer in Paisley, in 1847. John M'Arthur sold the subjects to
Mrs. Mary Millar or M'Donald, wife of David
M'Donald, sewed muslin manufacturer, Glasgow.
Mr. and Mrs. M'Donald granted a security over
their properties, Nos. 11, 12, and 13 of the
street, and the creditor brought them to sale.

James Caldwell,
successor to
William Barr.

Mr. James Caldwell, writer in Paisley, purchased
the property for behoof of the Commissioners of
Police, to make the spacious street. Mr. Caldwell was brought up with, and became the successor of, the late Mr. William Barr in his profes-
sional business. Mr. Barr was the gentleman
mentioned in the introduction, as being the chief
if not the only person pressing forward a similar
movement fifty years ago. Mr. Caldwell was a
Bailie and Commissioner of Police when the
movement for the present projected new street
commenced in 1866, and he entered into it with an
enthusiasm for street improvement as sanguine as
Mr. Barr did half-a-century ago.

END OF FIRST LECTURE.

II.

𝔅𝔩𝔞𝔨𝔥𝔬𝔩𝔢, 𝔅𝔩𝔞𝔨𝔥𝔬𝔦𝔩𝔩, 𝔅𝔩𝔞𝔠𝔨𝔥𝔬𝔩𝔢.

NOW,

Nos. 113, 114, 115, & 116 Causeyside Street.

———

 WILL now take up the lands of Blackhole, and commence with the original
Charter by giving the principal parts
thereof.

"*Carta Andree payntor*

"*Omnibus hanc cartam visuris rel audituris Robertus
pmissione dina Abbas mostij de pasleto et eiusd loci
conventus orlinis cluniacen glasguen diocs : Slatem
in dno semptna Noveritis nos hito sup hoc prius
diligenti tractatu viilitate mostij nri vndique pmsa
cu concensu et assensu tanq capti nra capitulat
congregat dedisse concessisse et ad feodifirma dimississe
et in hac pnte carta nra confirmasse Nec non dare
concedi et ad feodifirma dimitte et hac pnti carta
nra confirmare p delecto familiaris scutari nro Andree
ros alias payntour heredibs suis et assigti totum et
integrm illud tenementu quod vlgarit vocatr le blakhole Jacen in burgo nro de pasleto ex pte australi
eiusd trans torrente sancti myrini pr dtm torrente
contiue ex pte boreali eiusd ex pte vna continen ex
illa pte sup torrente triginta sex ulnas cu dimedia
vlne tendens versus occidente in longitudine Et tenementum Johannis logane ex pte australi ptibus ab
altra continen ex pte illa etia triginta sex ulnas et
demedm vlne Et sic ptem et medio erit descendens
versus boream et occidentem tamqe in trianguli
parte predicti habens antiori fronte publicu via regia
sine coem plateam burgi ad oriente continen in illa
pte in anteriore fronte quinquagita septe vlnas et
dimedm vlne et sic ascendendo et descendendo in*

Charter of
Blakhole.

longitudine et latitudine recto termite cu suis metis divisis et limitate et sic continen in toto in se et terram quaqe demedia roda quatuor decem le fawis et duas vlnas tre: In cuj rei testum sigillum coe capte nri huic pnte carte nre est appensu apud mostm nrm antedict quinto die mesis februarij anno dni milesio quindrasio tertio cora huius testibus nobiles viri Johani mungmry Jacobo halyburton magris de mungury et dyrrilton magro Alex Schaw rectore de cardross canonis Glasguen Roberto Sympill de foulwod John brown et Allan Stewart ballivis burgi de pasleto et Roberto Caveris cum diversis aliis."

Translation.

TRANSLATION.

"CHARTER OF ANDREW PAYNTOR.

"To all who shall see or hear this Charter, Robert, by divine permission Abbot of the Monastery of paslay, and Convent there, of the order of Cluny, in the diocese of Glasgow, Greeting in the lord everlasting, know ye that we have, after diligent enquiry, for the utility of our monastery on all points provided, with consent and assent of our chapter, chapterally assembled, to have given, granted, and in feu farm let, and by this our present Charter confirmed, Likeas, we give, grant, and in feu farm let, and by this our present Charter confirm to our beloved buckler servant, Andrew ros or payntor, his heirs and assignees, All and Whole

Description of Blakhole tenement.

that tenement which is vulgarly called the Blakhole, lying in our burgh of paslay, on the south side of the same, beyond the burn of Saint Myrin, between said burn, continuing on the north part of the same, on one side, containing from that part over the burn, thirty-six and a-half ells, stretching towards the west lengthways, and the tenement of John Logan, on the south side, also containing on that side thirty-six and a-half ells, and thus partly and medially it will come down towards the north and west, in the form of a triangle aforesaid, having in front of the king's highway and public street on the east, and containing in that fore front fifty-seven and a-half ells, and thus ascending and descending in length and breadth, in a right line, with its measures, divisions, and limits, and thus containing in itself, in whole every way, half a rood, fourteen falls, and two ells of land: In Witness whereof, our common chapter seal has been hung to this our present charter, at our monastery aforesaid, the fifth day of the month of february, in the year of our lord one thousand five hundred and three, before these witnesses, these noble men, John montgomery and James halyburton, masters of montgomery and dyrrilton; master Alexander Schaw, rector of Cardross, canon of Glasgow; Robert Sempill of fowlwood; John brown and Allan Stewart, bailies of the burgh of paslay; and Robert Cavers, with several others."

5th February, 1503.

Abbot Robert Schaw was nephew of the previous Abbot George Schaw. Abbot Robert was elected on the resignation of his uncle, on 14th March, 1498, and was promoted to the See of Moray in 1524. He was a good and excellent man, attentive to his ecclesiastical duties, and promoting the welfare of the people.

Abbot Robert Schaw.

In the Charter of the Unhouss, granted in favour of Andrew Payntour, on 18th May, 1490, he was designed burgess of Paisley; and in another charter of an acre of ground in Priorscroft, dated 18th June, 1490, he was also designed burgess. In other four charters, where he was one of the witnesses, he was likewise designed burgess. In an instrument of appellation, between Robert Schaw, Abbot of Paisley, and Lord Robert Blacader, Archbishop of Glasgow, taken in the *chapel of Saint Mirin*, Paisley, on 14th August, 1500, Andrew Payntor and Richard Brigton are the two last of seven witnesses. From references in other charters, it appears that Andrew Payntor and Andrew Ros or Payntor is one and the same person. In the Charter of Excambion of the Ladyhouse, between Abbot Robert Schaw and

Andrew Payntour, the vassal.

John Stewart, James Pantor is one of the witnesses. In the year 1521, Sir Thomas Pantor was prior of the Monastery of Paisley; and in 1528, James Pantor obtained license from Abbot Hamilton to dispose of the same acre of ground in Priorscroft that belonged to Andrew Payntor. I would suppose that Thomas and James Pantor were both sons of Andrew Payntor,—the one an ecclesiastic and the other a layman.

The name Blakhole.

In the description of the property it is stated that it was "vulgarly called the Blakhole." There is no indication whatever how it was called by that name, and it will therefore be a matter for conjecture whether it was originally a hermit's cave or hole, the *squalor carceris* (the prison) of the Monastery, or the pit or hole of the regality for drowning women convicted of theft, or a hole for steeping lint or tanning leather, or a low-lying angle of marshy ground occasionally overflowed by Saint Mirin's burn. It would be observed from the chapter on the "Ladyhouss" in Saint Mirin's-wynd, that the tenement granted to John Stewart was called the "Ladyhoill" or Ladyhouss. It is obvious there were holes on both sides of Saint Mirin's burn,—the one on the north side called *Ladyhoill,* and the other on the south side called the *Blackhoill.* The latter hole must have been dark when it obtained that black name. From whatever cause the tenement obtained the name of Blackhole, the subsequent lairds of these lands considered it a very honourable designation, for both the Stewarts and the Hamiltons called themselves of Blakhole for a century and a half.

Boundaries of Blakhole.

The property of Blackhole is described as bounded by Saint Mirin's burn on the north, which burn I have already noticed in chapter first. By the tenement of John Logan on the south. The charter of John Logan has been omitted to be entered in the Chartulary. By the king's highway and public street on the east, but it is not named. And the property having three sides, it is stated to be in the form of a triangle.

The witnesses to the sealing of the charter were,—1st. John Montgomery, master of Montgomery. He was the second son of Hugh, third Lord Montgomery and first Earl of Eglinton (his elder brother, Alexander Montgomery, having died in 1498, unmarried). John, master of Montgomery, was one of the parties engaged on the side of the Earl of Arran in the street conflict in Edinburgh, on 28th April, 1520, commonly called "Cleanse the Causeway," between the Earls of Arran and Angus, and he was killed in the affray, along with other seventy-one persons. 2nd. James Halyburton, master of Dyrrilton. He was the son of the deceased Archibald Halyburton of Dyrrilton, and Helen Schaw of Sauchie, sister of Abbot Robert Schaw. James, master of Dyrrilton, afterwards succeeded his grandfather, and became 5th Lord Halyburton of Dyrrilton. 3rd. Alexander Schaw, Rector of Cardross and Canon of Glasgow, was a relation of the Abbot. These three persons must have been on a visit to Abbot Robert Schaw when that charter was sealed, which is the only charter granted that year. 4th. Robert Sempill of Fulwood. This gentleman has been more frequently a witness to the sealing of the Abbot's charters than any other person. 5th. John Brown was a bailie when the charter was sealed, and also in 1508 and 1509. He was proprietor of the tenement now No. 99 High-street. 6th. Allan Stewart was also a bailie in 1503 and 1513. He obtained a charter on 16th May, 1490, from Abbot George Schaw, of the Orchard or Great Garden. The Orchard contained six acres and one perch of land, and extended from the property, now No.

Witnesses to the Charter.

Masters of Montgomery and Dyrrilton.

K

Abbey garden and wall.

12 Causeyside, to Gordon's-lone. The population of the Burgh at that time would not exceed 510, and the Orchard was entitled to be called the Great Garden. Abbot George Schaw had previously laid off a new garden around the Abbey, and enclosed it with an ashlar stone wall of a mile in circumference; and to commemorate the great undertaking, he put a mural tablet into the wall, bearing the following inscription in *alto-relievo :—*

Mural Inscription.

> " Ya callit ye Abbot georg of schawe
> about yis abbay gart make yis waw
> A thousande four hundereth zheyr
> Auchty ande fywe the date but weir
> pray for his saulis salbacioun
> yat made thus nobil fundacioun."

The whole of the inscription can be seen at the present day, with the exception of the fifth line, which a vandal has chiselled off. 7th. Robert Cavers. He was one of the first Bailies of Paisley in 1489. He feued the lands of Sclatersbank and a tenement in Priorscroft, on 2nd November, 1489. Sclatersbank was afterwards called Caversbank, for the Bailie, and remains Caversbank at the present day. The feu-duty of Blackhole was 6s. 8d.

John Logan's property.

In a charter of John Logan's property, granted on 17th July, 1517, by Abbot Robert Schaw to Nicol Steward, it is described as one acre and a half of land and four falls, containing in the front upon the street 16 rods 1 ell on the east, and so going down to the rivulet of Saint Mirin, between the land formerly Andrew Payntor on the north part and the land formerly Hugh Mershell on the south part. From that description in Nicol Steward's charter, it would appear that Andrew Ros or Payntor was not the owner of Blackhole in 1517, but it is not stated who had become the

new proprietor.   However, the Rental of Mortifi-
cations to the altar dedicated to Saint James and
Saint Nicolas (" Paisley Magazine," p. 526), dis-
closes the fact that "the yard callit blakhoill
" occupeit be umqle Wm. Stewarde gallowhillis
" payis zeirlie xvis."   The charter in favour of
William Stewart of Blackhole is not amongst
those in the chartulary; but I found another
charter granted by Abbot John Hamilton on
28th April, 1541, of the property now 29 High-
street, formerly the Salutation Inn, now the
North British Inn; in favour of "William
Steward de Blakhoill," which not only shows he
was proprietor of Blakhoill, but that he considered the name such an honourable designation
that he was called of Blakhoill.

William Stewart, of Blakhole, was also tenant
of the lands of Gallowhill, and he was appointed
a Bailie of Paisley in 1541 and 1542.   In 1557,
his son, William Stewart, who succeeded his
father, was desirous of disposing of part of the
lands of Blakhole; and on 12th January of that
year, John Hamilton, Archbishop of Saint
Andrew's, legate of the whole kingdom of Scotland, Abbot of the Monastery of Paslay, granted
to William Stewart, son and heir of the deceased
William Stewart, special license to feu to James
Bard, his heirs and assignees, one piece of land,
called his tenement in Blakhoill, lying in the fore
front of the same, containing in length 12 ells,
and in breadth 6 ells, for building. On 18th July,
1559, Archbishop Abbot Hamilton granted a
charter of the lands of Gallowhill to Elizabeth
M'Gie, relict of the deceased William Stewart, in
life-rent during her widowhood, and to the said
William Stewart, his son, in fee.   This is the last
charter, in the second volume of the Chartulary
of the Monastery, granted by the last Abbot of
Paisley before the Reformation of 1560.

(margin notes) Blakhoill.

Lands of
Gallowhill.

Commencement
of weaving trade
in Paisley.

Wobsters,
Weavers, and
Manufacturers.

Linen cloth.

Fancy fabrics.

The reformation and suppression of the Monastery of Paisley deprived the inhabitants of their usual means of support, for they were mostly servants and dependents on the Abbey. They had consequently to betake themselves to other business and employments; and the ecclesiastical Burgh being an inland town, they adopted the trade of weaving. At that early period, and for a century afterwards, the workers in that art were called wobsters, in the following century weavers, and in the next century manufacturers. The population of Paisley would not exceed 700 in 1560, and the wobsters were principally located in the west end of the burgall land, then called the Townhead. The Townhead extended from the West Port of Paisley (now 35 on the south side and 83 on the north side of High-street) to the Vennel, now called Lady-lane. Weaving was carried on in the Townhead for a considerable period, and as the population increased, buildings were erected in Causeyside, and the textile trade moved in that direction. The cloth originally made was coarse harn and plain linen, afterwards variegated with dyed yarn, wrought in stripes at first, and afterwards chequered; the fess cheque in the arms of the town of Paisley being the original armorial bearings of the Burgh, as seen sculptured on the head end of the Altar Tomb in the Sounding Aisle, and also sculptured on the armorial stones of the original Grammar School of 1586, and of the Meal Market of 1665,—the last of which is now in the Museum,—and impressed on the tokens of the Laigh Kirk of 1739 and 1784, and in William Semple's plan of Paisley. Burns, the national bard, in his admirable work of "Tam o' Shanter," takes notice of the extremely fine and beautiful fabric of Paisley, called seventeen hundred linen. Lawns, gauze, and muslins followed in every variety of texture and pattern that ingenuity and fancy could devise. The trade next developed into the enchanting manufacture of imitation Indian shawls, which in several instances surpassed the original. The town of Paisley at that time excelled every other place both in weaving shawls and weaving poetry ; and James Maxwell, one of the fertile rhymsters of Paisley, in his poem " On the Noble Art of Weaving," says, " Such matchless works are nowhere to be found—

" As here in Scotland, and in Paisley town,
   This may be noted, for its high renown,
   With other parts adjacent, which have learned
   Of Paisley, and with Paisley are concerned."*

On 8th March, 1584, John Stewart, son of William Stewart of Blackhoill and Gallowhill, was proprietor of a tenement and garden called *Hessilden*, which lay on the opposite side of Causeyside from Blackhole, and he, with consent of his father, feued the tenement of Hazleden to John Baird and Janet Allasoune, spouses ; and in warrandice thereof, William Stewart, the father, conveyed his two barns, lying between the lands at the end of the yard of William Stewart of Caversbank, called the *Nether Bailzie*, on the south part, and the lands and yard of the said William Stewart of Gallowhill, on the north and east parts. This is the first occasion on which I have discovered the words *Nether Bailzie* being used, which are not mentioned in Nicol Steward's

Hessilden,

and

Nether Bailzie.

* Since writing the above reference respecting the early manufacturers of Paisley, Mr. William Cross, formerly of Paisley, now of Glasgow, delivered a lecture in this Hall (Free Public Library) titled "Descriptive sketch of changes in the style of Paisley shawls," which was afterwards printed in the *Gazette* newspaper, Jan. 27–Feb. 10, 1872. It is the best essay I have read on the subject, and bears internal evidence of having been prepared by a Paisley practical weaver, an eminent manufacturer, and a gentleman of literary talent.

Mr. Wm. Cross, manufacturer.

The Knoll.

charter of 1517, neither mentioned in the charters of Hugh Merschell and Andrew Ross or Payntor, the conterminous proprietors on the south and north. The lands of Hessilden, when they were originally feued by Abbot George Schaw in 1493, were called the *Knoll.* The lands of Knoll, or Hessilden, on the east side, rose very abruptly from the ford of Saint Mirin's Rivulet, and the road therefrom eastward along the banks of the River Cart to the Wauk Mill belonging to the Monastery, was called Water Brae. The Wauk Mill was situated near the east end of Forbes-street, and was occupied by John Slater, fuller, the first fenar after the village was erected into a Burgh. Several members of this Slater family, down to the Reformation, were monks in the Monastery. The roadway at the ford of Saint Mirin's Burn, noticed in the previous lecture, would be seven feet lower in 1584 than it is at the present time.

Stewarts of Nether Bailie and Caversbank.

From the mortification to 'the altar of Saint James and Saint Nicolas, it appears that William Stewart of the Mill was proprietor of the lands now known by the name of Nether Bailie ; and from the charter of Hessilden, conveying the two barns in warrandice, it also appears that William Stewart of Caversbank was then proprietor of Nether Bailie. William Stewart of the Mill was the father, and William Stewart of Caversbank was the son. The latter was appointed a Bailie of Paisley in 1562, and he died in 1595. He was succeeded by his nephew, William Stewart, both in Nether Bailie and Caversbank. On 9th June, 1597, Helen Maxwell, relict of the deceased William Stewart of Caversbank, instituted an action in the Burgh Court against William Stewart, then of Caversbank, brother's son and heir to her husband, the said William Stewart. William Stewart having died, he was succeeded

by his son, James Stewart, who had married
Bessie Hamilton, sister of Margaret Hamilton,
spouse of John Wallace, commonly called the
"Guidwife of Ferguslie." Bessie, like her sister
the guidwife, refused to attend the Presbyterian
Kirk, and the Presbytery of Paisley appointed
Mr. Henry Calvert, minister of the Abbey, to
deal with her. The minister commenced dealing
with her on 30th June, 1642, and afterwards proceeded by admonition for the first, second, and
third times ; also by prayer for the first, second,
and third times ; but she being deaf to all
entreaties and the fulminations of the Church, he
ultimately, in February, 1645, excommunicated
her. James Stewart was succeeded by his son
James, and he died previous to 1678. On 3rd
July, 1678, the grandson of the guidwife of Ferguslie, William Hamilton of Ferguslie, lawful son
of John Hamilton of Bar, obtained decreet of
adjudication against John Stewart, son and apparent heir of James Stewart, of the lands of
Nether Bailie, for payment of £640 13s. scots.
John Hamilton of Bar, in Lochwinnoch parish,
eldest son of the said John Wallace, assumed the
name of Hamilton instead of Wallace. William
Hamilton assigned the decreet of adjudication
to Margaret Stewart on 11th June, 1680, and
she sold it to Neil Snodgrass, writer in Paisley,
on 1st March, 1697, and he obtained a Charter of
Adjudication of the lands of Nether Bailie, on
26th September, 1698. His name is entered in
the Poll Tax Rolls for 1695, for Renfrewshire,
page 55,—"Mr. Neil Snodgrass nottar publick,
"and pror of inferior court, 4 lib 6 sh., Anna
"his daughter 6 sh., Robert Alansone prentice
"6 sh., Janet Snodgrass servant 20 mks fie
"6 sh. 8d., £5·10·8." Mr. Neil Snodgrass
acted as agent for the panels in the trial for
Witchcraft at Paisley in 1697, when seven poor

*Case of
malignancy.*

*Case of witch-
craft.*

deluded creatures were convicted, and six of them worrit and burnt on the Gallowgreen of Paisley. The seventh, John Reid, had been imprisoned in Renfrew Prison till the day of execution, and he committed suicide, to save himself from the excruciating punishment of burning; and Dr. John Campbell of Paisley, and a Bailie (father of Robert Campbell mentioned in the previous lecture), gave it as his opinion, from the position in which Reid was found, "that some extraordinary cause had done it." ("History of the Witches of Renfrewshire," page 164). In 1698, Mr. Snodgrass was agent in a case in which Mr. William Reid, surgeon, was a party, and the latter having made some slanderous remarks concerning the former, respecting the witches case, Snodgrass raised an action of damages against Reid. (*Paisley Magazine*, page 154). Mr. Snodgrass was chosen Senior Bailie of Paisley in 1716 and 1717, and William Reid a Bailie in 1731 and 1732. Neil Snodgrass died in 1718, leaving an only son, John Snodgrass, a minor, who succeeded to several properties in Renfrewshire and Ayrshire. He afterwards bought the lands of Cunninghamhead in Ayrshire, in 1724. He was a successful agriculturist and improver of husbandry in Ayrshire. He sold the lands of Nether Bailie to Hugh Walkinshaw in 1740. It would seem, from the original charters, that these lands were not originally called Nether Bailie, and did not receive that name till a century afterwards. Mr. Gavin Lang, late Town-Clerk of Paisley, who took great pleasure in perusing the old documents under his custody, and also those coming through his hands, always maintained that the words "nether baillie" was a clerical error for "nether pasley," and that he had seen it written "nether pasley," and that the mistake, having been committed, the subsequent servile copyists continued it.

Margin notes:

Case of defamation.

Nether Pasley.

Having now disposed of the adjoining ground of Nicol Steward, called Nether Bailie, I will return to the lands of Blakhole.

On the death of William Stewart of Gallowhill, he was succeeded by his son, John Stewart, the proprietor of Hessilden, both in the lands of Gallowhill and Blackhole, and he died before 1596. On 7th February, 1596, John Fyfe, flesher, instituted an action against Janet Cunningham, relict and executrix of umquhile John Stewart of Gallowhill, and John Pirrhie, then her spouse. On 20th October, 1598, John Dicsoun, demster, servant to Dame Anabel Murray, Countess of Mar, raised an action of removing against William Stewart of Gallowhill, Margaret Stewart his dochter, John Pirrhie, Jane Cunningham his spouse, and two others, then tenants and occupiers of the waist tenement and yard therein described. That waist tenement in which the laird of Gallowhill and Blackhole, his daughter, mother, and stepfather resided, was the tenement which occupied the site between the properties Nos. 26 and 29 High-street, through which the street called "New-street" was made in 1736, for a road to the Laigh Kirk. William Stewart alleged a right to the property, and the demster of the Countess of Mar was decerned to give a letter of reversion to John Stewart, grandson of the said William Stewart. The countess of that day was Anabel Murray, daughter of Sir William Murray of Tullibardine, and Dowager of John Erskine, Earl of Mar, and Regent of Scotland. The Countess had been governess of the young King James VI.; and his Majesty, with John, Lord Erskine, her son, and Master James Sempill, apparent heir of Beltrees, were educated together, by the learned George Buchanan, under the eye of the Countess. On 18th June, 1600, Margaret, dochter of Gallowhill, was decerned to pay 5s. 10d.

L

Marginal notes:

Stewarts of Blakhole and Gallowhill.

Action of removing.

Schoolfellows of King James VI.

scots to Agnes Wilson and Robert Bailie, her spouse, for ail taken by Margaret two years bygone. The said Margaret Stewart was given up as a debtor in the testament of Bailie John Wallace, wine-dealer, who built the house now No. 29 High-street, Paisley, long known as the Salutation Inn, presently called the North British Inn. That property was the one feued by William Stewart of Blackhole, in 1541, afterwards belonged to Andrew Knox, minister of Paisley, who, on being appointed Bishop of the Isles, in 1605, sold it to Mr. John Wallace, and the present house upon it was built by Bailie Wallace in 1608. It may be inferred that Margaret Stewart was a good customer for wine and ail,—the common beverages for Scotland in these days. Patrick Stewart, Burgess of Paisley, son of the laird of Gallowhill, with consent of his wife, disposed of the lands of Blackhole in the year 1617. The lands of Blackhole, consequently, had been in the hands of the Stewart family for one hundred years. The lands of Gallowhill followed next; and the Stewarts, lairds of Blackhole and Gallowhill, are now totally unknown.

Claud Hamilton, Laird of Blakhole.

Claud Hamilton, burgess of Paisley, acquired the lands of Blakhole on 4th January, 1617, and are described,—" All and Haill the waist tenement "of land and yaird, and south yaird callit the "blackhoill;" and he immediately thereupon took the designation of Claud Hamilton of Blackhoill, by which he was called in all documents. He was chosen a bailie of Paisley in 1621 and 1634, and other five intervening years. He appears to have taken a deep interest in the municipal affairs of the Burgh, and he acquired several other properties in different parts of the town. He died in the year 1642. With the view of showing the astuteness of Bailie Hamilton of Blackhole, I may mention that he had a bachelor servant of

the name of John Morrison in his employment.
John Morrison had a few savings past him which
he wished invested in a small property, and
accordingly the Bailie purchased for him a house
next to the Hessilden on 22nd March, 1625. The
destination in the disposition was taken in favour
of the bachelor servant, his future spouse, what-
somever, if he any should happen to have, and
to the longest liver of them two, in conjunct fee,
and to the heirs lawfully to be procreated betwixt
them; whom failing, to James Hamilton, second
son of the Bailie, and his heirs and assignees.
John Morrison continued a bachelor, and died
unmarried. James Hamilton predeceased his
father's servant; and John Hamilton, his elder
brother, succeeded to the house as heir of provision in conquest on 30th June, 1646. Bailie
Hamilton's daughter, Marion Hamilton, married
Robert Alexander of Blackhouse, Town-clerk of
Paisley, who will be particularly noticed in the
fourth lecture, on "Paslay Tak." On the death of
Claud Hamilton, he was succeeded by his eldest
son, John Hamilton, and he immediately took
the designation of the lands,—John Hamilton of
Blackhoill. He was infeft, along with his wife,
Ann Cunningham, in liferent, on 18th December,
1642. He also succeeded to a tenement further
up the Causeyside, near the Common-lone, now
called Canal-street; and also to lands in Sneddon-
dyke, now Nos. 27 and 28 Back Sneddon-street,
and Nos. 52 and 53 Love-street. He was twice
elected a Bailie of Paisley, namely, in 1662 and
1663. His eldest son, Claud Hamilton, was married
to Elizabeth Sempill, and the father was a party to
their contract of marriage, and conveyed to them,
and the longest liver of them, in fee, the lands of
Blackhoill and the *Unhouss.* Claud Hamilton
predeceased his wife, Elizabeth Sempill, on 4th
January, 1673; and she, as longest liver, succeeded

Marginal notes:

Destinations of
Property.

Marion Hamilton
and Robert
Alexander.

Claud Hamilton
and Elizabeth
Sempill.

to both properties. Claud Hamilton had died in debt, and Patrick Carswell, notary in Paisley, a creditor, obtained a charter of adjudication on 13th April, 1676, on a decreet of adjudication, at his instance, against John Hamilton, son and heir of the deceased Claud Hamilton. The lands of Blackhoill only continued in the Hamilton family for fifty-six years.

Succession of Elizabeth Sempill, and her marriage with John Maxwell.

Elizabeth Sempill or Hamilton having become the proprietrix of Blackhoill and Unhouss, in virtue of her contract of marriage with Claud Hamilton, she shortly thereafter married John Maxwell, cloth merchant at the Cross of Paisley. He had become so enamoured with the name of his wife's property, that he designated himself John Maxwell of Blackhole. John Maxwell, in

Tailors' Society of Paisley.

1662, became a member of the Tailors' Society of Paisley; and the following year he was elected one of the two key-keepers or treasurers of the society, and kept the accounts for that year. In November, 1670, the government of the society was altered, by the addition of six ruling masters or managers, and he was elected the first master. In 1674, Maxwell borrowed 200 merks, and in 1677 another 100 merks, from the society. Francis Sempill of Beltrees and John Maxwell of Blackston became his cautioners. The old minute book of the Tailors' Society is now in the Reference Library, and I exhibit it in order to show the handwriting of John Maxwell.

Ezekiel Montgomery, Sheriff Depute of Renfrewshire.

In 1679, Mr. Ezekiel Montgomery of Weitlands, Sheriff Depute of Renfrewshire, obtained from Maxwell and his wife a disposition or right to the property, which was described as that waste tenement of land, of old called Blackhole; and about the same time he acquired Patrick Carswell's debt and adjudication. Mr. Ezekiel Montgomery, also in 1679, acquired from Hugh Fork of Merksworth, Sheriff Clerk of Renfrewshire, the reversionary interest of the Wood of Darskaith, then called New Yairds, and also the lands of Woodside. The Sheriff Depute dropped his title of *Weitlands*, and adopted that of *New Yairds*, leaving Woodside in abeyance. Mr. Ezekiel Montgomery was the son of James Montgomery of Weitlands, who was the son of Ezekiel Montgomery of Weitlands, who had purchased that small estate from the Sempills in 1625; and Ezekiel, the Sheriff, was also the grand nephew of Captain Alexander Montgomery, author of "The Cherrie and the Slae." Mr. James Montgomery wrote the first history of Renfrewshire about 1648 and 1650, mentioning, for the first time, the ridiculous and absurd story of the Cæsarean birth of King Robert II., which history will be found in the *Paisley Magazine*, p. 312. Mr. Ezekiel Montgomery was married to Miss Elizabeth Wemyss, of the Parish of Auchenderran, Fifeshire, in May, 1674, and he and his wife were infeft in Blackhole, on 24th January, 1682, and he was designed in the instrument of Sasine, Ezekiel Montgomery of New Yairds.

New Yairds and Woodside.

John Maxwell, notwithstanding the right he had given to Mr. Ezekiel Montgomery of the property, considered that he was still the proprietor, and exercised acts of ownership. Both Maxwell and Montgomery were in desperate circumstances at the time; and, from the crimes which they committed, both the claimants to the property were worthy of the name which it bore— the Blackhole. I will first take up the character of Maxwell, and then that of Montgomery.

John Maxwell and Ezekiel Montgomery, claimants to Blakhole.

John Maxwell, of Blackhole, was chosen senior Bailie of Paisley at the municipal election at Michaelmas, 1681. The Bailie considered himself a business man, and so proficient in writing (a specimen of which I have already shown to you in the minute book of the Tailors' Society), and

Bailie Maxwell of Blakhole.

Forgery by, and imprisonment of, Bailie Maxwell.

New election of a bailie.

Liberation of the bailie by a second forgery.

Capture of Bailie Maxwell.

particularly in signing his own name, that he took it upon himself to sign the names of other persons to pecuniary obligations, without asking their consent. Such obliging conduct on the part of the Bailie brought him into difficulties; and, in return for such kindness, he was accommodated with lodgings in the tolbooth for the crime of forgery. Placed in such a disagreeable position, and deprived of his liberty, he was unable to perform his official duties of Bailie; and the Privy Council issued a commission in May, 1682, to the Town Council, "to meet and elect a Bailie in place "of John Maxwell, whose place they declared "vacant, from certain misdemeanours committed "by him." The Council met on 27th May of that year, and elected John Snodgrass, maltman (mentioned in first lecture), in his stead. The imprisoned Bailie, however, perceived a mode of escape under the bill of indemnity, in favour of a certain class of covenanters, and ingeniously argued with himself that, if by signing other peoples' names he was thrust into prison, he might by signing other persons' names be liberated from prison. The Bailie accordingly wrote a protection under the Indemnity Act, and signed the King's name and that of the Secretary of State, the Earl of Moray, to it. The Bailie, who was imprisoned in jail for forgery, also by forgery was liberated—a pure and persecuted covenanter. John Adam, who had been elected a Bailie in September, 1682, and deacon of the Tailors' Society in November the same year, resigned the former; and on 27th December following, John Maxwell, late bailie, was elected in his place. In November, 1682, the Tailors' Society resolved to prosecute the representatives of Beltrees for payment of Bailie Maxwell's debts and whole interest from their dates, Bailie Maxwell not having paid anything. The Privy Council afterwards

discovered that the Bailie had used and produced a false protection, and he, being
charged before the Privy Council on 27th
May, 1683, alleged he had lodged a true Protection, and that some persons must have abstracted
it and lodged the protection exhibited in its
place. The Bailies were allowed a proof, and the
witnesses deponed the very reverse of his statement. On 1st December, 1684, the Tailors'
Society sold their debt against Bailie Maxwell
and the representatives of Beltrees and Blackston, to Bailie Robert Pow,—the latter stipulat-
ing that if he was unsuccessful in recovering the
price from the representatives of Francis Sempill
and John Maxwell of Blackston, the two deceased
cautioners, he was to be repaid 10 lbs. scots.
Bailie Maxwell, considering that he was still
owner of Blackhole, obtained license from Bailie
Pirrhie to cast five score of rigging turves for his
fore house, of the tenement called Blackhole.
On 26th November following, the whole tenants
in the property were warned to remove at Whitsunday, 1686, at the instance of Elizabeth Sempill and her husband, John Maxwell ; on 26th
January, 1688, Mr. Ezekiel Montgomery and the
whole tenants were warned to remove, at the
instance of the Bailie and his wife, at Whitsunday following ; and again, on 29th January, 1690,
the warning was repeated against the same parties, at the same instance.

I shall now take up the conduct of Mr. Ezekiel
Montgomery, Sheriff Depute of Renfrewshire.
On the 10th of April, 1682, he caused the effects
of Bailie Maxwell to be poinded, who was highly
indignant at such an affront ; and on the following day, John Fork, writer in Paisley, became
cautioner for the late Sheriff Depute, that he
should produce, betwixt and the 16th then instant,
the letters of horning and poinding under which

Ezekiel Mont-
gomery's disputes
with Town
Council.

he poinded Bailie Maxwell, and that under a
penalty of 500 merks scots ; and if he failed in
the production, the Burgh fiscal was authorised
to prosecute.   The Town Council held a meeting
on 19th April, 1682, presided over by Bailie Maxwell, and after ratifying the Acts of the Burgh
respecting common lands, the minute proceeds,—
" And the said Robert Landess fiscal, &c., having
" complanit to the said bailie and counsell fore-
" said, upon Mr. Ezekel Montgomerie, lately

" sheriff deput, for calling the councell convenit
" in the tolbuith, on the 19th of this instant,
" ane pack of beasts and sumphs, for the coun-
" cell's requiring the said late sheriff depute to
" produce the letters of horning and poinding
" quhairwith he had poinded bailie Maxwell,
" conforme to ane act of cautioune fundin be
" him, for productione of the letters of horning
" and poinding forsaid, under the penaltie of five
" hundredth merks money of fyne, upon con-
" sideratioune of the quhilk misbehaving words
" spoken before the councell, the said bailie and
" councell ordains that upon sight ther officers
" apprehend the said Mr. Ezekel Montgomerie
" wherever he can be apprehended within the
" townes jurisdictione, ay and whill sufficient
" cautione be found be him, that he sall ansr the
" fiscall as law will, and to be emprissoned qll
" he find catioune to the efft. forsaid."

On the 29th of the same month, another meeting of Council was held, respecting information
they had received of Mr. Ezekiel Montgomery
going to Edinburgh to raise a summons against
the town, and empowered Bailie Maxwell and the
Town Clerk to follow him to Edinburgh, and
watch his motions, and drew a precept on the
Treasurer, Andrew Cochran, to advance the
Bailie forty pounds Scots to pay his expenses.   A
difficulty, however, arose from the Treasurer re-

fusing to pay the cash ; but the Council advanced it. Bailie Adam and several of the Councillors were afraid of the legal proceedings threatened by the late Sheriff Depute, and entered into an arrangement with the Sheriff, and called and held a meeting of Council on 8th May, 1682. The meeting repudiated the arrangement of Bailie Adam and his colleagues, on the ground that Bailie Maxwell and the Town Clerk, Mr. Snodgrass, had been in Edinburgh at the time, and ratified the previous act of Council.

At a meeting of the Privy Council, held on 14th February, 1684, Mr. Ezekiel Montgomery of Weitlands, Sheriff-Depute of Renfrew, being pursued for twenty-four articles of malversation, oppression, concussion, and extortion from the poor people at the last Circuit Court, 1682, to squeeze money to himself, Sir William Paterson, and Mr. Thomas Gordon, clerks,—such as seizing on a woman's goods on pretence she was going to hang herself, because her head was found fettered in a net hanging down from the bedhead, and taking away 1000 mks. of money from a man whose house was burned accidentally ; but in seeking among the rubbish he found that bag, and he told the people that he had not lost at all, for he had recovered so much of his money ; but Mr. Ezekiel took it from him, on the pretext that it was a hid treasure and pose, and so belonged to him as Sheriff. The High Treasurer urged that Mr. Ezekiel should find caution, under the pain of £1000 stg., to abide all the diets of process, and not to flee before sentence. He offered caution, which being insufficient, he was committed to prison. At another meeting of Privy Council, held on 13th March, 1684, the King's Advocate insisted that Ezekiel had obtained money from twenty persons, at granting certificates of their having taken the test before him, whereas several

Meetings of Privy Council.

Extortions of the notorious Ezekiel Montgomery.

M

Liberation of Sheriff Montgomery on his agreeing to become King's evidence.

His flight to Ireland,

and

his return to Paisley on the eve of the Revolution, 1688.

of them never could write, and others of them refused to take it. He was liberated on Alexander, 2nd Lord Blantyre, becoming cautioner in 1000 mks. ; but on Ezekiel being set at liberty, he fled, and was apprehended in the Pleasants, beside the Cowgate Port of Edinburgh, and imprisoned. On 2nd April, 1684, a letter from the King was laid before the Council, indemnifying Ezekiel as to life and fortune, notwithstanding the depending process against him, provided he ingenuously discovered what he knew of the accession of any heritor to the late rebellion, or anent their resetting such, or of the unlawful extortion used in the Circuit Court, and assoilzied him from the libel. They let him out on bond, and then he ran away to Ireland and beguiled them. On 21st November, 1684, the case of Mr. Ezekiel Montgomery was called before the Privy Council, and he failed to appear (it being stated he had become a preacher in Ireland). He was denounced fugitive. A few years now passed away, and coming events were casting their shadows before. Murmurings of discontent, deep and serious, had been prevalent during the licentious reigns of Charles II. and James VII.; distant sounds of impending revolution were becoming clearer and louder ; fugitives from political crimes were returning to the kingdom ; and the weak and waning Government saw its end approaching. Amidst the noise of people's voices, the throes of a sinking dynasty, and a universal cry for liberty, the bold and imperious late Sheriff-Depute returned to Paisley, not being afraid of the Government he had beguiled. Mr. Ezekiel Montgomery on his return sold his lands of New Yairds and Woodside on 10th September, 1688, to Thomas Crawfurd of Cartsburn, the father of George Crawfurd, the historian of Renfrewshire ; and he, again, disponed them to his second son, Thomas Crawfurd, on 30th July, 1692. Thomas

Crawfurd, and all the succeeding proprietors of these lands, discarded the title of New Yairds, used by Sheriff Montgomery, and restored the ancient title of Woodside. He sold the lands of Blackhoill on 26th October, 1692. In the Poll Tax Rolls for 1695, page 61, his mere name, "Mr. Ezekiel Montgomery," is entered; and from the position on the roll, it appears he was residing in Blackhole, but no sum was attached to his name.

Sale of Woodside and New Yairds.

The next proprietor of the lands of Blackhole was Robert Ross of Robinshill, serviter to William, Lord Ross; and in the Poll Tax Rolls, page 74, he is entered "Robert Ross, chamberlain to Lord "Ross, heritor, 100 and below 200 lib val 4 lib "6 sh, Elizabeth Aichesoun spouse 6 sh, George "Francis and Agnes children each 6 sh, "Alexr. Dunloup servt 18 lib fee 9 sh, Agnes "Greer and Marion Crawford each 16 lib fie 8 sh "each, £7 13sh." Mrs. Ross was probably a sister of Mr. John Aicheson, co-Sheriff Depute along with Sheriff Montgomery. Sheriff Aicheson was also imprisoned along with Sheriff Montgomerie in 1684, but it does not appear any further proceedings were adopted against him. In 1704, a dispute arose between Robert Ross and Hugh Crawfurd of Woodside, son of Thomas Crawfurd the former proprietor, respecting a room in the Abbey Church. Mr. Crawfurd claimed the seat as the Woodside room in the church, and Mr. Ross claimed it in virtue of an assignation from Mr. Ezekiel Montgomery in 1695. The complaint came before the Kirk Session, who ordered Mr. Montgomery to produce his original right to it, and he having failed to do so, the session confirmed the room to Woodside. In May, 1703, Robert Ross granted an annuity of 120 lib scots, out of his lands of Robinshill, to James Dunlop of Househill. Robert Ross also purchased other lands, and he died about the end of the year 1707.

Robert Ross of Robinshill.

Double sale of a church seat by Ezekiel Montgomery.

George and
Francis Ross.

He was succeeded by his eldest son, George
Ross, writer in Paisley, who died in 1709, and
he was succeeded by his brother, Francis Ross,
merchant in Paisley. The affairs of Francis Ross
became embarrassed, and he granted bonds over his
property of Blackhole, the Unhouss, and all his
other properties. Three adjudications for debt
were also obtained against him and the Blackhole
property. All these bonds and adjudications
were acquired by James Fulton, surgeon in
Paisley, the owner of the lands of Orchyard, on
the opposite side of Causeyside, a younger
brother of Bailie Robert Fulton. Both the bailie
and the surgeon were men of wealth, and great

Bankers of
Paisley in 1730.

money-lenders,—the Bankers of Paisley in these
days ; and in looking into the bundles of title
deeds of their period, either the one or the other
of them would be found to be the absolute owner
of, or the bondholder over, the property. James

Old Orchard of
the Abbey.

Fulton feued out the lands of Orchyard, and
formed Orchyard-street in a line with New-street
in 1743 ; a very narrow street, only twenty feet in
breadth. The reason assigned for its narrowness
has been said to have arisen from Bailie Fulton,
his brother, being unable to see the propriety of
wasting ground for a broad street, when it might
be better applied at the back of the houses for
kail-yards. James Fulton died on 14th November,
1746, aged 55 years, and left legacies to several
charitable institutions and corporations in the
town. In 1732, the affairs of Francis Ross had
come to a crisis, and he, with consent of Dr.
Fulton, sold Blackhole in two portions.

Division of the
lands of Black-
hole.

The southmost half (Nos. 113 and 114 Causeyside)
was bought by John Renfrew, smith in Paisley
(noticed in first lecture), the purchaser of No. 9
Saint Mirin-street; and the northmost half (Nos.
115 and 116 Causeyside) was bought by William
Dougal, wright in Paisley. The lands of Black-

hole, which gave a title to the old proprietors, the Stewarts and Hamiltons, have now been parcelled out ; and the word "Portioner," which is occasionally seen added to a proprietor's name, shows that he is not an heritor, but only an owner of a portion. The southmost half of Blackhole lands is not to be touched with the new street, and I will confine myself to the northmost portions, which have been purchased by the Commissioners of Police for the formation of the spacious opening.

William Dougall again subdivided his half into two portions, and sold the southmost half (No. 115 Causeyside) to Robert Corse, of Wallnook of Paisley, on 29th September, 1753. Mr. Corse had previously purchased the lands of Greenlaw about 1738. He was descended from the family of Corse, who occupied the Corsemilne on the Levern, it is said, for the long period of 400 years. In the Transept of the Abbey, there is a tombstone with the following inscription :— *Sub-division of Blackhole lands.*

> " THIS IS THE BURIAL PLACE OF
> JOHN CORS Cors MILN 1460."

And upon another stone in the chancel :— *Burial place of the Corses.*

> " THE BURIAL PLACE OF JNO
> CORSE, CORSEMILN, 1691,
> AND ROBERT CORSE MERCHT
> OBT SEPT 1777 ETATIS 76."

The last is Robert Corse of Geeenlaw.

The property was next acquired by Alexander Walkinshaw, weaver in Paisley, and William Walkinshaw, stockinger in Seedhill there, on 10th January, 1756. Alexander Walkinshaw was the father of Robert Walkinshaw, of Parkhouse, writer in Glasgow, and, for the long period of forty-seven years, Sheriff-Clerk of Renfrewshire, from 1785 till 1832. These parties sold the property to William Borland in 1760, whose trustees sold it to James Richmond in 1817, and his *Successive proprietors.*

trustees to the Merchants' Society of Paisley in 1832. The Merchants' Society had previously become proprietors of the adjoining property, 114 Causeyside, and they purchased the present property for the protection of the lights of the other. The front house, built after the great fire, was only one storey high, and thatched. The society immediately, in 1833, sold the subjects.

Wm. Galloway, an enterprising townman.

Mr. William Galloway, manufacturer, Paisley, next acquired the subjects, under certain restrictions as to building; and the new proprietor, an enterprising manufacturer, had the primitive thatched building pulled down, and the present excellent three-storey tenement erected on the site, for the purpose of carrying on the business of a shawl merchant, in which he had become engaged. Mr. Galloway had a strong desire for geological pursuits, particularly searching for the Black Diamond, in which he was ultimately successful at Barleith, Hurlford. Mr. Galloway died on 12th March, 1854, in the 51st year of his age; and there is a tombstone erected to his memory in the Paisley Cemetery.

Robert Rowat, a successful manufacturer.

The subjects were next acquired by Robert Rowat, manufacturer, Paisley, — a successful man of business, who, in his young days, carried on a considerable trade in what was called thibet shawls, from the name of the yarn. Mr. Rowat having made a competency, retired to his villa at Prospecthill, and left the business to his three sons. He died on 26th March, 1869, aged 78. Mr. Robert Rowat, the oldest son, succeeded to the property, and he has sold it to the Commissioners of Police for the street improvement.

Building over St. Mirin's Burn.

William Dougal retained the northmost half, and in 1732 purchased from William Wallace of Caversbank a small portion of the lands of Unhouss, and from William Greenlees also a small portion of his property in Saint Mirin's-wynd, to enable him to build over Saint Mirin's Burn. I may here remark that Andrew Ross or Payntor, who was original feuar of the lands of Blackhole in 1501, from Abbot Robert Schaw, had a right by his charter to build over Saint Mirin's Burn, but that old charter was totally unknown in 1732. A house was rebuilt on the property after the great fire.

Nathaniel Forrester, dyer, a young man about twenty-three years of age, proposed to purchase the subjects from William Dougal, and after considerable trouble, he bought the property at 900 mks. (£50 sterling), with half-a-guinzie of gold paid down to Janet Hardie, the seller's wife. It would seem that the laird was very difficult to deal with, and that the young purchaser from the country enlisted the sympathies of Mrs. Dougal, by promising and paying a gold half-guinea to her, that he might acquire the subjects on the burn for his trade of a dyer. In 1744, he acquired more ground from William Wallace, the proprietor of the Unhouss, for the purpose of extending his business. Nathaniel Forrester, laird of Arngibbon in Stirlingshire, and dyer in Paisley, afterwards married Janet Maxwell, youngest daughter of Gavin Maxwell of Castlehead, and they were both infeft in the property in 1751. Mr. Forrester died at an early age, as appears from a tablet inserted in the wall of the Chancel of the Abbey,—

Nathaniel Forrester of Arngibbon, and dyer in Paisley.

" This is the burying-place of NATHANIEL FORRESTER, Maxwellton, who died July 24th, 1756, aged 39 years, and Janet Maxwell, his spouse, who died October, 1777, aged 58 years; and of Janet Downie, their grand-daughter, spouse of Andrew Barrie, Paisley, who died 20th May, 1800, aged 29 years; also, of Benjamin Downie, who died 24th January, 1806, aged 19 years; also, of Mrs. Mar-

Tombstone of the Forrester family.

garet Maxwell Forrester, relict of Benjamin Downie, Esq. of Blairgorts, Stirlingshire, who died 18th April, 1831, aged 88 years; also, of the said Andrew Barrie, who died 30th January, 1837, aged 91 years."

Downies of Blairgorts.

In 1778, Margaret Forrester, spouse of Benjamin Downie of Blairgorts, in the parish of Kippen ; Janet Forrester, spouse of Alexander Gibson, writer in Paisley ; Agnes Forrester, spouse of Robert Wright, merchant there ; Mary Forrester, spouse of Bailie Andrew Brown, manufacturer there, and Bethia Forrester, indweller there, made up and completed titles as heirs portioners of their father. Two of Margaret Forrester's children rose to great eminence in Spain, as the following obituary notices will show :—

Natives of the town rising to eminence in Spain.

" Died at the Royal Palace, Seville, on 5th June, 1826, his Excellency Sir John Downie, Major-General in the army of his Catholic Majesty, Commandant-General of the Province of Andalusia, Governor of the Palace of Seville, and Knight Grand Cross of the Military Order of Saint Ferdinand. His remains were interred the following day with all the honours corresponding to his civil and military rank."

"Died at Madrid, on 4th June, 1843, Col. Charles Downie, in the service of the Queen of Spain, last surviving son of the late Benjamin Downie, Esq. of Blairgorts, Stirlingshire."

Alex. Gibson, Town-Clerk.

Alexander Gibson, husband of Janet Forrester, afterwards became Town-Clerk of Paisley, on 11th November, 1768, and in 1780 he built the self-contained house No. 44 High-street, which he called Townhead House. His son, Nathaniel Gibson, succeeded his father as Town-Clerk, and he occupied the same house, and died on 17th February, 1827, aged fifty-eight. Robert Wright of Whiteside, husband of Agnes Forrester, was a tobacconist, and he was also owner of property in High-street, with large garden behind, and built the houses Nos. 31 and 32 High-street. His son,

Nathaniel Wright, who succeeded him, sold the large garden to Mr. Peter Kerr, on which the Free Saint George's Church and other buildings have been erected. Andrew Brown, husband of Mary Forrester, resided in New-street, opposite the Laigh Kirk, and commenced business as a manufacturer on 3rd December, 1753. The block of buildings in New-street and Shuttle-street bear the date of erection 1737, when these streets were laid off for building; and the latter street bears ample evidence in its name that it belonged to the ancient weaver town. His daughter, Jean Brown, by his first marriage, married Mr. William Sharp, who was assumed a partner in the business, which was then carried on under the firm of Brown & Sharp. In the list of eighteen manufacturing firms given by William Semple, in his "History of Renfrewshire," page 323, this one is entered "Brown, Sharp, & Co., wareroom, New-street;" and in the Paisley department of the Glasgow Directory for the following year, 1783, "Messrs. Brown & Sharp, manufacturers, New-street." In the London Directory for 1789, they are entered "Brown, Sharp, & Co., gauze weavers, 16 Bread-street, London;" and in the London Directory for 1871, "Brown, "Sharps, & Tyars, muslin manufacturers, 18 "Watling-street, E.C." In the first Paisley Directory, published in 1810, "Brown, Sharp, & Co., manufacturers, Shuttle-street;" and in that for 1871, "Brown, Sharps, & Tyars, muslin "manufacturers, 166 George-street, and 18 "Watling-street, London." This is the oldest manufacturing firm in Paisley,—is still carrying on business,—and has weathered all the fluctuations that have occurred during the last 118 years. On a tombstone erected in the High Church cemetery, there is the following inscription :—

" Erected in 1837, by Andrew Brown, in memory

Side notes: Bailie Brown. — Brown and Sharp, manufacturers. — Andrew Brown's tombstone.

of his uncle, who died at Funchal, 22nd February, 1787 ; Andrew Brown, his grandfather, who died 22nd March, 1806; Mary Forrester, his grandmother, who died 10th November, 1812 ; Andrew Brown, his father, who died 20th October, 1836."

His mother, Joan Kirkwood, died on 5th December, 1871. Bethia Forrester, commonly called Beatrix, married Thomas Stevenson, merchant in Paisley. He built the large incle or tape factory in St. James-street and Caledonia-street. He assumed his son, Nathaniel Stevenson, as a partner. The tape manufacturing was not vigorously carried on by the son after the father's death, dwindled away, and was given up about forty years ago, when the buildings in St. James-street were converted into dwelling houses, and those in Caledonia-street were some time occupied as a hand-loom weaving factory, and now as a potatoe dealer's store. In the Abbey cemetery there is a tombstone with the following inscription :—

" To the memory of Thomas Stevenson, merchant in Paisley, who died 26th July, 1815 ; and of Beatrix Forrester, his wife, who died November, 1795. This monument of filial affection was erected by their surviving son, Nathaniel. MDCCCXV."

The Forresters and their husbands sold the property to John Paton, weaver in Paisley, in 1779, for £180. He also purchased small pieces of ground from the proprietors on the north side of the burn in 1794, and in 1795 took down the old building and erected the present house of polished ashlar front, consisting of a sunk storey for cellarage, three flats above, and a *Nepus* thereon. Houses with a nepus was a style of architecture very prevalent in Paisley in the year 1780, and must have been much admired at that time, from the number that is to be seen in different parts of the town. A *nepus* was an expensive erection, very unremunerative, from the

Marginal notes:

Incle or tape factory.

Stevenson's tombstone.

John Paton.

Nepus architecture.

first cost and the annual repairs required. It
was generally adopted at a period when hundreds
of houses were erecting in town, to lodge the
thousands of immigrants flocking from other
places to share in the high wages allowed for
weaving; but that style of architecture, like
some of the fancy fabrics of the place, scarcely
survived its introduction. In 1771, the population **Population.**
of Paisley was 5000; and in ten years thereafter,
1781, it had leaped up to 16,000; and in other
ten years, 1791, to 20,000. John Paton executed
a Deed of Settlement in 1798, conveying his property to his children, John, Matthew, and James
Paton. Their descendants sold it in 1853.

A portion of Paisley Abbey towering above the **West front of**
surrounding buildings is visible from this part of **Paisley Abbey.**
Causeyside, and the venerable building is an
object that never loses its interest in the eyes
of the inhabitants of the town and stranger
visitors. It has frequently formed the subject of
the poet, the painter, and the photographer; and
I may be pardoned in referring to one of
the painters on the present occasion. In
1828, the then Burgher old meeting-house
situated in Abbey-close, directly opposite the
Abbey, was taken down for the purpose of erecting a modern and more commodious church. On
the removal of the old building, which had stood **Removal of**
sixty years, one of the grandest views that could **Abbey-close**
be imagined of the magnificent western gable of **meeting-house.**
the Abbey, was opened up from Causeyside.
Measures were immediately taken by a number
of townsmen for preserving permanently the temporary view that had been thus obtained of the
beautiful Gothic architecture of the receding
doorway and the windows, with their mullions
and tracery. Several hundreds of pounds were
subscribed to purchase another site for the new
church, but the requisite amount not being ob-

James Cook's painting of Abbey from Causeyside.

tained, that project, like many other proposed improvements in Paisley, fell to the ground. The new erection was accordingly commenced on the old site; but Mr. James Cook, landscape and portrait painter in Paisley, fortunately made a painting of the elaborate Gothic gable, taken from Causeyside, in front of the property No. 116, for the purpose of preserving on canvas the temporary view. The Painting was afterwards lithographed and published, bearing the following inscription :—

PAISLEY ABBEY.
This View from Causeyside is Respectfully Inscribed to
THE REV. R. MACNAIR & THE REV. P. BREWSTER,
By their obedient Servant,
J. COOK.

The lithograph, in which I take somewhat of a personal interest, from having one early summer morning seen Mr. Cook taking the sketch for his painting,—and of which I possess a copy,—recently caught my eye, and I took it down to examine it. The foot of Causeyside and Saint Mirren's-street form the foreground. I observe a dyer's barrow wheeling up Causeyside filled with yarn, and a carrier's van emerging from Saint Mirren's-street making for the manufacturers' warehouses. On the right side of the picture is the portly form of old John Hart the jailor, in his knee breeches and rig-and-fur white stockings, standing on the street, speaking to a gentleman on horseback, and attended by his two faithful greyhounds. John Hart was a great courser, and was generally admitted to keep the best-trained greyhounds in the West of Scotland. On the left side is the corner of the once famous Turf Inn. The Turf was in its day a well-known rendezvous for the traders of the district and the travellers who came to Causeyside by way of business. Farther in the picture, on the same side, is bustling Betty

John Hart and his greyhounds.

Turf Inn.

Boyd, fruit and vegetable dealer, superintending the sale of her goods, which were always exposed in the eddy or corner of the street between the foot of St. Mirren-street and the river—the corner being then much more commodious than since the erection of the existing buildings, when the street line underwent considerable deviation. Mr. Cook in his day occupied a highly respectable position as a local artist, and I happen to be the fortunate possessor of one of his *chefs d'œuvres*, "The Conversion of Saul." Mr. Cook died 26th November, 1841, in his 49th year. The Messrs. Cook of the *Gazette* newspaper are two of his sons.

Mr. Cook's painting of the conversion of Saul.

John Kerr, manufacturer in Paisley, acquired the property No. 117 Causeyside, the northmost portion of the Blackhole, in 1853. He commenced business in 1810, assumed his brothers as partners in 1812, and then carried it on under the firm of John Kerr & Company. The company removed from Causeyside to Saint Mirren's-square, at the ends of Brown's-lane and Shuttle-street, afterwards called George-place. In the *Paisley Directory* for 1823, by Robert Biggar, they are entered, "John Kerr & Co., Saint Mirren's-square ;" and in the next published directory for 1827, by George Fowler, "John Kerr & Co., George-place." William Lyon, the celebrated stage-coach driver of the "Sons of Commerce" between Paisley and Glasgow, occupied part of the premises for coach-yard and stabling, and he is entered in the Directory for 1823, "William Lyon, coach-setter, Saint Mirren's-square." He was succeeded by his manager, Mr. James Stewart, now station-master at the Caledonian Railway Station, Buchanan-street, Glasgow, as tenant of the premises in *Saint Mirren's-square.* The mere mention of the name of Saint Mirren's-square brings to my recollection other circumstances connected with it almost forgotten, but of importance

John Kerr, manufacturer.

Saint Mirren's-square.

Saint Mirren's mill.

in the town at the time they happened. The premises were originally erected for a cotton spinning work, and called "Saint Mirren's Mill," from the burn of that name being the north boundary; and the business was carried on under the firm of M'Kerrell, Laing, & Company, cotton spinners. Between 1819 and 1823, the old mill was converted into a barracks, for soldiers brought into the town to quell the Radical risings of 1819 and overawe the weavers of Paisley in their demands for Parliamentary Reform and redress of their grievances, by the presence of the "red-coats." On the new barracks at Williamsburgh being erected, and Saint Mirren's-square vacated by the martial men, the premises were then occupied by a firm whose senior partner was one of the most peaceful men of Paisley. Messrs. Kerr & Company removed in 1830 to Abbey-street, and continued in business till 1850. Mr. John Kerr, the owner of the Causeyside property, was one of the unobtrusive gentlemen of Paisley, and died a bachelor. He did not engage in political squabbles. His highest ambition was to lead a quiet life, and he died in peace, in 1857, at the age of 75, without an enemy. At the division of Mr. Kerr's properties, the one in Causeyside was allotted to his sister, Mrs. Barr, and her family, and they sold it to the Commissioners of Police for the formation of the new street.

The name of the tutelary Saint of Paisley has been very seldom connected with business. The first occasion I am aware of was that of "Saint Mirren's Mill," in Saint Mirren's-square; and the latest is that of "Saint Mirren's Soapwork." The latter name has become celebrated throughout the country in connection with the soap; but, from the modern spelling used, has caused many persons in distant places to suppose the Saint was a female,—the washerwoman of the Abbey,—and

Saint Mirren's soap-work

adopted as the *Patroness* of cleanliness. With the view of dispelling the feminine appearance of the name, and restoring the original and ancient orthography to the spacious opening, and giving the proper name of the PATRON Saint of the Abbey, I marked it on the plan I made of the old places, with the masculine name of the man,

"SAINT MIRIN PLACE."

SAINT MIRIN PLACE.

———

END OF SECOND LECTURE.

III.

The

Unhouss, Vnehouss, Ovenhouse,

Now, No. 14 Saint Mirren's Street.

—

HE tenement called the Unhouss was feued by Abbot George Schaw to Andrew Payntor, burgess of Paisley, on 18th May, 1490. The following is a copy of the principal parts of the Charter :—

" Carta Andree payntor

" Omnibus hanc cartam visuris vel audituris georgius pmissione dina abbas mostij de pasleto et eiusdem loci convtis ordis cluniacen glasguen diocs Saltem in dno sempitna : Noveritis nos habito sup ho prius diligenti tractatu utilitate de nro mostij vndqe pmsa et prefata cu consensu et assensu totis capte nr capitulari congregata dedisse concesse assedasse et ad feodifirma dimisse et in hac pnti carta nr confirmasse Nec non dare concesse assedas et ad feodifirma dimitte et hac pnti carta nra confirma delecto nro And payntour burgensi burgi nr de pasleto vnam perticatam tre burgalis cum pertinen jacen in dicto burgo nro que olim muncupata le vnhouss int tenementu nrm muncupatam le trewlis feu ex pte boreali ex parte vna et tenementum dicti Andree payntour ex pte australi ptibus ab alt et in fronte antrore continen sex vlnas ex pte australi et tot vlnas ex pte occidentali et sic indeferent in latitudine equaliter continen octo vlnas et sic ascendendo et distendendo p ptes sine fines nri tenementi qe le trewllis feu dr ac tenementi ipsius Andree nec non tenementi Johannis alexr cum omnibus suis rectē metas et mesuris antiquis et divisis In cj et testiom sigillu coe capti nri hanc huic

Charter of Un-houss granted to Andrew Payntor.

Description.

pnti carte nre est appensum apud mostij nro antdictum decem octavo die mensis maij ano dno millesio quadrages nonagesio cora huis testibus viz Roberto Sympill de fowllwood Johane quitfurde Jacobo crawfurde Roberto cavers Johane schaw Allan stewart dmi henrico mouss vicar of kilbrachan Alexander clugston psbtr et Jacobo yong notariis publici ac divers aliis."

Testing clause.

TRANSLATION.
"CHARTER TO ANDREW PAYNTOR.

"To all who shall see or hear this charter, George, by divine permission, abbot of the Monastery of Paslay and convent of the same place, of the order of Cluny, in the diocese of Glasgow, Greeting in the Lord everlasting, Be it known to you all, that we, upon diligent inquiry upon all points, and for the utility of our monastery, with consent and assent of our whole chapter, chapterally assembled, to have given, granted, assigned, and in feu farm let, and by this our present charter confirmed, Likeas we give, grant, assign, and in feu farm let, and by this our present charter, confirm to our well-beloved Andrew Payntour, burgess of our burgh of Paslay, one particate of burgall land, with pertinents, lying in our said burgh, which was formerly called the Unhouss, betwixt our tenement called the trewlis feu on the north part, on one part, and by the tenement of the said Andrew Payntour on the south part, on the other part, and in the fore front containing six ells on the east part, and as many on the west, and in breadth different, containing eight ells, and as many in ascending and descending, beyond the boundaries of the trewlis feu, and from the tenement itself of the said Andrew, and also the tenement of John Alexander, with the right bounds and ancient measures and divisions of the same: In witness whereof, our common chapter seal is hung to this our present charter, at our Monastery aforesaid, the eighteenth day of the month of May, in the year of our Lord one thousand four hundred and ninety, before these witnesses,—namely, Robert Sempill of Fowlwood, John Quhitfurd, James Crawfurd, Robert

Translation of the Latin charter

o

Cavers, John Schaw, Allan Stewart, Sir Henry Mouss vicar of Kilbarchan, Alexander Clugston presbyter, and James Young, notaries public, and several others. Feu-duty, 8s."

Derivation of Unhouss.

In the description of the subjects, it is stated that it was formerly called the Unhouss. *Un, une, oon* (Gothic), an oven; *hus,* a house; *un-houss,* an oven-house. In former times, previous to the date of the charter, the bakehouse or cook-house of the Monastery, or of the village of Paisley, must have been situated in the ground here feued, and would be superseded by the erection of the Refectory and other offices, beside the Monastery, by Abbot George Schaw in 1484.

Situation of the Unhouss.

The Unhouss or oven-house appears to have been situated between the tenement called the "Trewlis feu," on the north, and another tenement of Andrew Payntor, on the south. The word "*trewlis*" only occurs in this charter, and there is no charter to be found in the Chartulary granting the "trewlis feu" itself to any person by that distinctive name. There is, however, a charter granted on 10th September, 1498, by Abbot Robert Schaw, to "Richard

Feu to Richard Brigton.

"Brigton, burgess, his heirs and assignees, "heritably, of all and whole that our tenement, "lying and situated in our burgh of Paslay fore-"said, between the tenement of Andrew Pantor "on the south part, and the tenement of David "Alexander on the west part, and the common "mercat-place of the said burgh, as well on the east "part as on the north part,—this said tenement "containing in itself thirteen ells of burgal land in "front, on the north, and eight and one-half ells on "the south-east part." This feu of Richard Brigton does not appear in any of the subsequent charters of the venerable Chartulary of the Monastery. It may, however, have merged into the feu of the *Paslay Tak,* to be noticed in the fourth lecture.

The proprietors of the Unhouss and Blakhole were for a considerable period the same parties, and I will here only recapitulate the names of the successive owners. William Stewart acquired the subjects about 1517. He was succeeded by his son, William Stewart of Gallowhill; who was succeeded by his son, John Stewart of Gallowhill; who was next succeeded by his son, Patrick Stewart of Gallowhill. Claud Hamilton, burgess of Paisley, next acquired the subjects in 1617. He was succeeded by his son, John Hamilton.

Proprietors of "Unhouss" and "Blackhole."

I have now arrived at the stage when I am obliged to refer to the rentals delivered by Lord William Cochran of Paisley, to the Town Council of Paisley, on 3rd May, 1658, when they purchased the Superiority of Paisley. In the Pittance Rental (*Paisley Magazine*, page 685), will be found the following entry :—

Rental of the town, 1658.

"𝔇𝔢 𝔑𝔲𝔦𝔨 𝔥𝔬𝔲𝔰𝔰, 𝔬𝔣 𝔄𝔲𝔩𝔡 𝔠𝔞𝔩𝔩𝔦𝔱 𝔱𝔥𝔢
𝔙𝔫𝔢 𝔥𝔬𝔲𝔰𝔰, 𝔭𝔢𝔯𝔱𝔞𝔦𝔫𝔦𝔫𝔤 𝔱𝔬 𝔶𝔢 𝔰𝔞𝔦𝔡
𝔙𝔪𝔮𝔩𝔩 𝔚𝔪 𝔖𝔱𝔢𝔴𝔞𝔯𝔱 𝔊𝔞𝔩𝔩𝔬𝔴𝔥𝔦𝔩𝔩𝔦𝔰 𝔟𝔦𝔦𝔧 𝔰𝔥." .

Nuik house.

The house seems to have lost its ancient distinctive name of *Unhouss* with the public, and was at that time called, in the Scots language, the *Nuik Houss*,—that is, the house in the corner or angle, a very true description, for it is in the corner or angle at the present day. The writer of that entry has very properly explained that in ancient times the tenement was called the Vne Houss. John Hamilton conveyed the Unhouss and the Blakhole properties to his son Claud Hamilton and Elizabeth Sempill, by their contract of marriage, and to the survivor of them. Elizabeth Sempill was the survivor, and consequently became owner of the property. She afterwards married John Maxwell, merchant, as mentioned in the second lecture.

John Maxwell of Blackstoun.

John Maxwell of Blackstoun acquired the Unhouss from Elizabeth Sempill, relict of Claud Hamilton of Blackhole, with consent of her husband, John Maxwell, merchant, by disposition and assignation, dated 13th November, 1678. Blackston belonged to the Monastery of Paisley, and it is entered in the Rental Book of the Abbey, in the year 1460, as "in the hands of the Abbot for grange." Abbot George Schaw, at the time he was building the offices of the Monastery, and enclosing the new orchard or garden, erected a manor place on the lands of Blackston, on the banks of the River Black Cart, for a residence or a place of retirement from the fatigues of ecclesiastical duties.

Manor place of Blackston.

Abbot George Schaw resigned the Abbacy in March, and became a pensioner on the Abbey, as mentioned in the first lecture. John Hamilton, the last Abbot of Paisley, conveyed the temporalities of the Abbey to his nephew, Claud Hamilton, third son of the Earl of Arran, on 6th December, 1553. Claud Hamilton was then ten years old, he having been born in Blackness Castle, in September, 1543, where the Countess of Arran had been conveyed for greater security in these troublous times. These possessions were erected into a temporal lordship in 1587, in favour of the said Claud Hamilton, then Commendator, and he was created Lord Paisley on 29th July, 1591.. He died in 1621, aged seventy-eight.

Birth of Lord Paisley.

James, 1st Earl of Abercorn.

His eldest son, James, created Earl of Abercorn in 1606, repaired and enlarged the manor place of Blackston, probably for his own residence, during his father's lifetime, and whom he predeceased on 16th March, 1618. James, second Earl of Abercorn, succeeded his father and grandfather. About 1650, he sold the whole lands of the Abbacy inherited by him, and left Paisley. The Earl, when he sojourned here, resided in the Place of Paisley, which was to the south of the Abbey and Saint Mirin's Aisle. The Place is still entire, now fronts Abbey-street, and is occupied by Mr. Andrew Foulds, wine and spirit merchant, and several other tenants. The 2nd Earl's chamberlain or factor, John Wallace of Ferguslie, second son of William Wallace of Ellerslie, well known as the husband of Margaret Hamilton, commonly called the Guidwife of Ferguslie, occupied the Manor House of Blackston. Margaret Hamilton was the great grand-daughter of John Hamilton, who acquired Ferguslie in 1545, from Abbot John Hamilton, and she, being a Hamilton, had similar leanings to Popery, like her chief, Lord Paisley, Earl of Abercorn. The guidwife was a strong-minded lady, determined to exercise her womanly rights, by refusing to attend the ordinances of the Presbyterian Kirk. During the residence of John Wallace and the Guidwife of Ferguslie in Blackston Manor House, the Presbytery of Paisley instituted a process of malignancy against her for not attending the Parish Kirk of Paisley. Blackston is situated in the Parish of Kilbarchan; but she must have been considered a parishioner of Paisley for her lands of Ferguslie, and her husband attending the Abbey Church. The ecclesiastical proceedings were commenced in June, 1642, and continued till June, 1647, when she was carried on a wand bed from Blackston House to the Abbey Kirk, to listen to the ministrations of Mr. Henry Calvert, the minister of the Abbey.

Blackston lands and the manor place, and the lands of Middleton and Linwood, were acquired by Sir Patrick Maxwell of Newark, about 1650, when the Earl of Abercorn was disposing of his possessions. I would suppose the Laird of Newark and his eldest son George, immediately after the purchase, took up their residence in

Marginal notes:

Place of Paisley.

Guidwife of Ferguslie.

Blackston lands bought by Sir Patrick Maxwell

Kilbarchan register of births.

Blackston House, from the following entries in the register of births for the Parish of Kilbarchan :—

"19 August, 1653. The qlk day, Sir Patrick Maxwell of Newark, his daughter is baptized, named Jeane. Witnesses, Symon Birsbane of Selvieland, and John Maxwell of Southbar."

"30 December, 1653. The whlk day, George Maxwell, young laird of Newark, his son is baptized, named Patrick. Witnesses, Andrew Knox, brother-german to Ranfurlie, and Hew Semple, son to Noblestoune."

"30 Jany., 1659. George Maxwell, young laird of Newark, had a child baptized, called Jean. Witnesses, James Birsbane of Selvieland, and Alexander Hamilton."

"8 Sept., 1661. John Maxwell of Blackstoune, had a child baptized, named Katherine. Witnesses, James Birsbane of Selvieland, and Alexander Hamiltoune."

John Maxwell of Blackston.

Sir Patrick Maxwell would probably convey the lands of Blackston, Middleton, and Linwood to his son, John Maxwell, about the year 1660, who would immediately thereupon take up his residence at the manor-place of Blackston. Woodrow, in his "History of the Sufferings of the Church" (Vol. II., page 28), says, that on 28th November, 1666, the laird of Blackstoun, in the Shire of Renfrew, was present at a meeting of gentlemen at Shutterflat, near Beith ; but from the statements, it is difficult to say from his behaviour whether he was there voluntarily or kind of half-forced. The captain of the little troop was William Mure of Caldwell. Information having been received that Captain Dalziel was on the road, they wisely resolved to disperse. Maxwell, says the historian, to save himself from prosecution, gave information against the others. On 13th December, 1667, Maxwell of Blackston presented an application for liberation from Edin-

Meeting of Covenanters at Shutterflat.

burgh Castle, which was granted on his giving bond to keep the peace, under the pain of ten thousand pounds scots. Woodrow also states,— "It was remarked that after this Providence "frowned very much upon him, and everything "went cross. This he himself is said to have "acknowledged, in a paper he left behind him, "when a good many years after this he went for "Carolina; but he died at sea by the way." Many Scotsmen at that time took refuge in that settlement, and many of the Covenanters were banished to that country and sold to the planters. It appears from the Minute Book of the Tailors' Society of Paisley, that John Maxwell of Blackston died in 1684.

William Mure of Caldwell, commander of the little troop, fled to Ireland, and from thence to Holland, where he died of grief in the year 1670. His estates were forfeited and bestowed on that unrelenting persecutor, General Thomas Dalziel of Binns. Lady Caldwell and her daughters were reduced to poverty, imprisoned for attending conventicles, and suffered much for their firm adherence to the cause of truth. Binns is in the Parish of Abercorn, and the General was born there in 1599. He was a determined Royalist in the reigns of Kings Charles 1. and II. He served in the Russian army for ten years, and fought against the Turks and Tartars. He returned to the service of King Charles II. in 1666 ; and it is well known how the fierce zeal of the Cavalier and cruelty of his Muscovite training were displayed in his persecuting and oppressing the noble band of patriots and martyrs that maintained and secured civil and religious liberty in Scotland. Dalziel raised the Regiment of Dragoons on 25th November, 1681, afterwards called the Scots Greys. He died about Michaelmas, 1685, aged 86.

[marginal notes:] William Mure of Caldwell.

General Dalziel.

At the laying of the foundation-stone of Paisley
Grammar School and Academy, with Masonic
honours, on Saturday, 31st October, 1863, Robert
Brown, Esq., as Lord of the work, mentioned,
among other remarks, that William Mure of
Caldwell, when a boy, was educated in the
Paisley Grammar School. I find that young
Master Mure attended the Grammar School
from Candlemas, 1648, to Candlemas, 1650, under
the schoolmaster, John Knox. Master Mure

lodged with John Spreull, merchant, who resided
in his own property, now 26 High-street, Paisley.
Spreull belonged to the family of Coudon, in the
neighbourhood of Caldwell. If Master Mure was
taught grammar by a John Knox, the principles of
civil and religious liberty would be instilled into
his young mind by John Spreull and his wife,
Janet Alexander. John Spreull was six times
elected Senior Bailie of Paisley between the years
1648 and 1658. During that period, the most
powerful nobleman in the County of Renfrew,
Lord William Cochran, attempted to invade the
rights of the inhabitants of Paisley, and was
boldly met and defeated by Bailie Spreull. Bailie
Spreull also vindicated religious liberty, and was
fined in £360 for maintaining his principles. In
1667 a troop of General Dalziel's dragoons came
down High-street, halted at Bailie Spreull's house,
and commenced a search for him ; and, being
unable to discover his retreat, they threatened to
roast his second son, John, a boy of ten years of
age, unless he pointed out the hiding-place of his

father. He refused, and stood firm to his resolution not to disclose it. That boy, after he became
a man, endured many sufferings for nonconformity,
and was twice tortured before the Duke of York
and the Committee of Privy Council of Scotland,
the Duke of York remarking that " Mr. Spruell
" was more dangerous than five hundred common

"people." On 14th July, 1681, John Spruell, yr., was fined in £500 sterling, and imprisoned in the Bass Rock for six years. After his liberation, he was generally called Bass John Spreull. He commenced business in Glasgow, and had a large establishment at Crawfordsdyke, Greenock, for making red herring. He also became one of the adventurers, to the amount of £1000 sterling, in the joint-stock of the company trading to Africa and the Indies, established in 1696. George Crawfurd, the historian of Renfrewshire (Semple's edition, pages 5 and 183), called him, "My very "good friend, Mr. John Spreull, of Glasgow, "merchant, author of the ' Accompt Current "betwixt Scotland and England.'" Bass John was born in 1657, and died in 1722.

Catherine Maxwell, daughter of John Maxwell, and heiress of Blackston, was married to Alexander Napier, grandson of John Napier of Merchiston, the celebrated inventor of the Logarithms. From the register of baptisms for the parish of Kilbarchan, it appears that Alexander Napier and Catherine Maxwell of Blackston had a child baptised on 11th August, 1689, called John ; witnesses, Alexander Cunningham of Craigends, and Alexander Porterfield. Alexander Porterfield was the laird of Fulwood, and the second son of Porterfield of that ilk, married to Craigends's daughter Marion.

Robert Ross, serviter to Lord Ross, acquired the Unhouss property from John Maxwell of Blackston, in July, 1682, and it was described in his disposition—

"All and Haill ye tenement of land, high and laigh, back and fore, with the close yrof, and yeard adjacent yrto, on the south syde of ye King's hie street, betwixt the tenement of William Wallace, maltman, on ye east, Saint Mirrin's burn on ye south, ye tenement of Robert Alexander of black-

P

Marginal notes:

Catherine Maxwell Mrs. Napier.

Robert Ross of Robinshill.

house and of Robert Park yr on the west, and the hie street on the north parts."

He was succeeded by his son, George Ross, writer, and he again by his brother, Francis Ross, merchant, who are all mentioned in the lecture on Blackhole, to which reference is again made. Francis Ross sold Blackhole Lands in 1732, and the Unhouss in 1736. In 1733, the houses upon the Unhouss property were all burned to the ground, in the great fire of that year. The steading and the ruins were exposed to sale in the Tolbooth of Paisley on 26th August, 1736, by Francis Ross and James Fulton, the heritable creditor, and purchased by William Wallace of Caversbank, the maltman mentioned in the first lecture, for £24 sterling. The tenement is thus described in the conveyance to him dated 24th November, 1736 :—

Francis Ross, merchant.

" All and Haill that part of the tenement lying on the south side of the burgh of Paisley, consisting of 12 ells in front, within the walls, from the middle gavil of the same, with the cellar and office-houses on the east, and of the said tenement, as also a piece of yearding, consisting of 9 ells in breadth, at the head thereof, and of 5 ells in breadth at the foot of the same, being a part of that tenement of land, high and laigh, back and fore, with the closs and pertinents, lying on the south side of the King's high street of the said burgh, and bounded betwixt the tenement of the said William Wallace on the east, Saint Mirrin's burn on the south, the tenement which belonged to Robert Alexander of Newton and the heirs of the deceased Robert Park, Writer, on the west, and the King's high street on the north parts."

Great fire of 1733

Then follows a statement, that the tenement had been made ruinous by the fire which happened in the said Burgh on 2nd June, 1733. Similar statements are to be found in other conveyances of the burned tenements; and it must have been considered a very destructive conflagration, when it was thus noted in these documents, to preserve evidence of the fact. I have already referred to William Wallace of Caversbank leaving his heritable properties to his second son, James Wallace, to convey certain of these to the female children of his deceased brother, William Wallace. James Wallace, in obedience to that direction of his father, conveyed this property, in 1747, to Agnes Wallace, eldest daughter of William. In the disposition, the property was then described :—

"All and Haill that part of the tenement and yard called Blackhole, lying within the territories of the Burgh of Paisley, regality thereof, and Shire of Renfrew, bounded by the other part of the said tenement and yard, belonging to the representatives of the deceased David Rodger, wright, on the west, Saint Mirrin's burn on the south, his other tenement in Burngate on the east, and the King's high street on the north parts."

This is the first occasion on which the Unhouss, lying on the north side of Saint Mirin's burn, was called *Blackhole;* and since that time, it has been improperly called by that name. Blakhole, the subject of my second lecture, lay on the south side of Saint Mirin's burn, in Causeyside, but both properties had belonged to the same owner till 1732, with the single exception of John Maxwell of Blackston.

Agnes Wallace sold the subjects the same year, 1747, to George Cochran, wright in Smithhills of Paisley. He came from Cartside, in Kilbarchan parish, and retained the subjects till 1761; but he must have been in difficulties between these dates, from the numerous legal prosecutions against him. In 1761, he granted a trust deed in favour of James Wallace of Caversbank, Alexander Knox, brewer in Crawford's-dyke, and John Sym, wright in Paisley. In 1762, they sold the property to John Macfarlane of Auchinvennell in the parish of Row, for £220 stg., and he borrowed

Misnomer of Blackhole.

Several transmissions of the property.

£120 on security of the property. The following year, 1763, he exposed the subjects to public sale, and they were purchased by Patrick Adam in Garelochhead, the bond-holder. Macfarlane having died before he conveyed the property, the purchaser had to raise an action of adjudication in implement against Robert Macfarlane, the eldest son of the seller.

Purchased by John Miller and Thomas Bissland.

In 1765, John Miller, merchant, and Thomas Bissland, wright in Paisley, acquired the subjects. William Semple, in his "History of Renfrewshire," published in 1782, at page 331, says " there are four ancient houses which I will take " notice of by desire of a number of people." After mentioning three of these old houses, he says,— " The next land is the Blackhole, at the head of " St. Mirran's Wynd. It was acquired from " Elizabeth Semple, relic of Claud Hamilton, " November 30, 1678, by John Maxwell of Black- " ston ; it was acquired by William Wallace of " Caversbank, November 24, 1736 ; and is now " the property of Messrs. John Millar and " Thomas Bessland, who, *anno* 1765, re-built the " said house 5 stories high, where 6 families " live, each one perpendicular above another." The other three houses referred to by Semple were really old houses ; one had been erected in 1580, another in 1594, and the third in 1608. He has mentioned that the house then on the property at the head of Saint Mirran's-wynd was built in 1765, making it at the time he wrote only seventeen years old, while the previous house, built in 1746 by George Cochran, would have been only thirty-six years old ; and I would therefore suppose the historian must have referred to the house burned in 1733. At the time the tenement of 1765 was erected, it was the most conspicuous and handsome house in the town of Paisley,—the population at that time being 4600,—and will stand comparison with many modern buildings of the present day.* Before commencing building of the house, the owners applied to the Town Council, and were allowed to bring the house 7 feet forward on the street or oven-house angle, and that is the reason it projects beyond the two conterminous houses. In 1771 the two proprietors entered into a contract of division of the property.

Mr. Miller was the son of William Miller, of Dykes, Kilbirnie, and on the death of his father in 1753 he succeeded to the estates. On the birth of his first child he made the following entry in his memorandum book :—"Mary Miller was born "June the 13th day, and baptized the 24th of "the said month at Beith Kirk ; born under the "sign Cancer and the planet Mars, the 20th day "of the Moon, 1741." *[Birth of John Miller's first child]*

Mr. Miller was a great supporter of the Protestant succession and the House of Brunswick, and accordingly joined the Militia company raised in Paisley, in 1745, to oppose the Pretender's son. He was taken prisoner at the Battle of Falkirk, fought on 17th January, 1746. In the year 1768, he was elected Treasurer of the town of Paisley. After his death, a tombstone was put up in the Abbey Cemetery, bearing the following inscription :— *[Mr. Miller taken prisoner by the rebel army.]*

"This is the burying-place of John Miller, late merchant in Paisley, who died May 5, 1791, aged 80 years ; and Elizabeth Craig, his spouse, who died 14th September, 1779, aged 66 years." *[Old tombstone of John Miller.]*

In again mentioning the Militia company and the battle of Falkirk, it brings to my recollection, that in noticing in my first lecture, Andrew Lumsden, or Lumisden, as receiving the £500 of fine in-

---

* Robert Russell, Esq., has kindly taken a Photograph of this building; two views of Saint Mirren's-street,—one from the head, and the other from the foot, of the street; and a Photograph of the houses in Causeyside that are to be taken down. *[Photographs of houses to be taken down.]*

Fining of the town of Paisley by Prince Charles Edward Stuart.

flicted on the town of Paisley, on 30th December, 1745, by the Pretender's son, then in Glasgow, I omitted to state that the cash was paid to Andrew Lumisden. Three hundred pounds of the fine was raised and paid on Thursday evening, 2nd January, 1746, and an interim receipt granted by Lumisden to account; and the hostages, Bailie Matthew Kyle and William Park, were further detained till the following morning, when the balance was paid to Lumisden, the interim receipt returned, and the following receipt granted for the full amount :—

Receipt granted for the fine of £500,

and

protection to the town.

" CHARLES, Prince of Wales, &c., Regent of Scotland, England, France, and Ireland, and the Dominions thereunto belonging: To all the Inhabitants of the Town of Paisley; whereas, you have by the hands of William Park, merchant in Paisley, made payment to our Secretary for our use, the sum of five hundred pounds sterling, which we have accepted off, as the contribution laid upon you, in respect of your raising militia and otherwise opposing our interest, we therefore not only Grant receipt of the foresaid sum, but hereby Grant full and ample protection to you for your estates, houses, goods, merchandises, and effects of what kind soever, from all injuries, violence, or insults offered or done by any person or persons whomsoever; requiring all His Majesty's officers, civil or military, to see this protection inviolably observed. Given at Glasgow, the third day of January, 1746.

" By his Highness' Command,

The body of the receipt is in the handwriting

of John Goodwillie, another Edinburgh writer, who acted as clerk to Lumisden. Murray always wrote his name in tall letters. The letters of the name signed to the receipt are, however, taller and heavier, but bear a strong resemblance to his genuine signature. Lumisden wrote a small, neat hand. The morning on which the receipt was signed, Murray was confined to his room with a lame leg, and Goodwillie carried the receipt to him; and if Goodwillie signed the receipt, he would do it at the special request of Murray. In 1750, Goodwillie, from the respect he had for Lumisden, named a child after him.

Andrew Lumisden, the son of William Lumisden, writer in Edinburgh, was born in 1720, and brought up to his father's profession of the law. At 25 years of age, he joined Prince Charles Edward Stuart, and was appointed keeper of the Prince's Seal, and clerk to the Prince's Secretary, John Murray of Broughton. In the latter capacity, Andrew Lumisden carried the Prince's "sinews of war,"—the cash in the treasury bag. That Seal sealed the receipt for the fine of £500. After the rout of Culloden, on 16th April, 1746, Lumisden skulked about the Highland fastnesses for four months, carrying the Prince's Seal in his pocket, at the end of which period he came to Edinburgh, and afterwards went to London, travelling in disguise, passing several of his most intimate friends without recognition. He sailed from London in the latter end of the year for Rouen. In writing from Rouen, on 27th Nov., 1747, to his mother, desiring her to send him certain books and clothes, he particularly desired her to put in his own seal into the package, "*but not the Prince's Seal.*" Lumisden must have therefore left the Prince's Seal with his mother during the short time he resided in Edinburgh in disguise. Where is that Seal now? Connect-

Writer and subscriber of the receipt.

Biography of Andrew Lumisden, under-secretary and first clerk of the Prince's Treasury.

The Prince's Seal.

ing, as it does, the Prince and the keeper of his Seal with the town of Paisley, it must form an interesting object in the eyes of the admirers of "Bonnie Prince Charlie." On the Prince's expulsion from France in December, 1748, his followers were left destitute, and the French Government proposed to make provision for his faithful servants, and appointed a committee to examine their claims, and report. The report on

French report of Lumisden's character.

Lumisden's claim was,—" That he is a gentle-
" man ; was principal under-Secretary and First
" Clerk of the Treasury ; and to shew the con-
" fidence the Prince reposed in him, he entrusted
" him with the keeping of his Seals, to be in
" readiness when necessary." Lumisden (along with other thirteen persons) was admitted on the Gratification List, with an allowance of 600 livres annually. Early in 1751, Lumisden was appointed assistant-Secretary to the Chevalier de Saint George (King James VIII.) at Rome, with a small salary.

In July, 1753, the Town Council of Paisley raised an action in the Court of Session against

Action for repayment of the fine of £500.

John Murray of Broughton, the Pretender's Secretary, for repayment of the £500. Murray stated in defence that he did not sign the receipts for the money ; that his clerk, Lumisden, had forged his name to them ; and that he was relieved of all liability by his Majesty's Act of Grace, which extended to all persons who had surrendered in terms of it. The action was decided on 28th July, 1759, by a majority of the judges acquitting the defender. The veracity of John Murray could not always be depended on.

Lumisden, on the death of James Edgar, on

Lumisden appointed principal Secretary to the Chevalier.

24th September, 1762, was appointed principal Secretary to the Chevalier. The Chevalier died on 1st January, 1766, and Prince Charles Edward (the pretended King Charles III.) succeeded to the barren Crown, and continued Lumisden principal Secretary till 8th December, 1786, when he was dismissed, along with a number of others,—a circumstance very agreeable to them all, for they were tired of the manners of their King and his mock Court. Lumisden was allowed to visit England, and he came from Paris in 1773, and in 1788 obtained a full pardon.

Andrew Lumisden, fifty-two years after the Rebellion, published a quarto volume, of 478 pages, in 1797, titled, "Remarks on the Antiquities " of Rome and its Environs, illustrated with en- " gravings, by Andrew Lumisden, Esq., Member " of the Royal and Antiquary Societies of Edin- " burgh," which reached a second edition in 1812. He died suddenly at Edinburgh on 26th December, 1801, aged 81 years.

Lumisden's publication on the antiquities of Rome.

Miss Isabella Lumisden, only sister of the under-Secretary,—the fair Isabella, with white cockade and wreathed smiles,—recruited for the Prince's standard, in the Prince's Court held in Holyrood Palace. In 1747, she married Robert Strange, an engraver, who had been enlisted in the Life Guards of the Jacobite army. He afterwards studied at Rome, and acquired a European fame. On 5th January, 1787, King George III. waved a sword over the sculptor on bended knees, not to cut off his head, but to desire him to rise SIR ROBERT STRANGE, Knight. Sir Robert died 5th July, 1792, aged 71 ; and Lady Strange died on 28th February, 1806, aged 87 years.

Isabella Lumisden's attendance on the Court at Holyrood.

Her marriage with Robert Strange,

and

Knighthood of her husband.

What an interesting subject for a fine picture ! Bonnie Prince Charlie in the dining-room of the house of Colonel M'Dowall of Castlesemple, Glasgow (formerly the Shawfield Mansion, afterwards the residence of John Glasford of Dugaldston, a native of Paisley, and partner with Alexander Speirs of Elderslie), attended by his secretary,

Subject for a picture ! Prince Charles, his secretaries, and Paisley bailies.

Q

Murray, and his clerk, Andrew Lumisden, impos-
ing a contribution of a thousand pounds on the
town of Paisley; and old Bailie Kyle, seventy-
five years of age, and venerable William Park,
seventy-eight years old, with their snow-white
locks, pleading the poverty of the Burgh, and
humbly beseeching the Prince for a reduction of
the vast amount !

Biography of
Thomas Bissland.

Thomas Bissland, the other co-proprietor of
the *Unhouss* property, came from Drymen to
Paisley along with his younger brother, Alexander
Bissland. They were both wrights, and commenced business in Paisley. Their father before them was a wright; and their elder
brother, John, who was also brought up a wright,
remained in Drymen and succeeded to his father's
business, which his descendants are carrying on
at the present time. Thomas Bissland, in 1760,
entered into partnership, in the timber business,
with Charles Maxwell of Merksworth, when Paisley was expanding rapidly,—when house after
house was being built, and street after street
being laid off, in the west part of the town called
Broomlands, and the east part called the Abbey
Garden,—the Abbey Garden being the garden
formed by Abbot Schaw in the year 1484. The
company carried on an extensive business in timber, trading to and from the Baltic and the Mediterranean in their own ships. The building of houses
at that time, and for the following period of forty
years, was a prosperous trade, and the company
of Maxwell & Bissland had its full share of the
prosperity. Thomas Bissland was appointed Town
Treasurer in the year 1771. He was married to
Margaret Kibble, and in 1785 he purchased part
of the lands of Whiteford called Auchentorlie.
Thomas Bissland died previous to 1804, and was
buried in the cemetery of the Abbey, where the
spot is pointed out by a stone, bearing the in-

scription, "This burying-place belongs to Thomas "Bissland, merchant in Paisley, 1785." He left a son, Thomas Bissland, jun., merchant in Paisley, born 29th March, 1772; and two daughters, Elizabeth Bissland, wife of William Stuart of Gryffe Castle, merchant, Paisley, and Miss Janet Bissland. Alexander Bissland, formerly mentioned, was the father of the late William Bissland, manufacturer, who resided in Orr-square.

Thomas Bissland, jun., in 1798, purchased from John Gibb, innkeeper, in Paisley, part of the lands of Ferguslie, on which he had erected a house, and the adjoining ground on the east, called Sergeant's Acre. Mr. Bissland made additions to the house, and also altered it to the castellated appearance presented at the present day. The ancient road that leads past Ferguslie House had by that time become a private road, from the new public turnpike road further south having been opened up. The old road was then popularly called the "Wood-road," from its leading to the bonnie wood of Craigielee by the service roads to the old quarries of Ferguslie. On Thomas Bissland, jun., succeeding to his father, he designed himself of Auchentorlie; and, in 1806, he purchased from the Town Council of Paisley the remaining lands of Ferguslie, consisting of 156 acres of ground, at the price of £12,000. The "Wood-road," "Sweet Ferguslie," and the "Bonnie wood of Craigielee," must have been dear spots to our modest, tender-hearted lyric poet. Tannahill, who wrote with sympathetic feeling from the heart to the heart, penned four epitaphs, one of which he said was

Thomas Bissland, junior, of Ferguslie.

"FOR T. B., ESQ.,

"A gentleman whom indigence never solicited in vain.

"Ever green be the sod o'er kind Tom of the Wood !
    For the poor man he ever supplied ;
We may weel say, alas ! for our ain scant of grace,
    That we reck'd not his worth till he died :

Tannahill's epitaph on Thomas Bissland, junior.

Though no rich marble bust mimics grief o'er his dust,
  Yet fond memory his virtues will save ;
Oft at lone twilight hour sad remembrance shall pour
  Her sorrows, unfeign'd, o'er his grave."

Philip Anstruther Ramsay, the editor of the edition of the poet's works published in 1838, in a note, says,—"This benevolent individual still sur-"vives. The allusion in the first line is to Ferguslie "wood, which is elsewhere celebrated as a favour-"ite haunt of the author's." Epitaphs are generally written after the death of the individual; but to the above the editor has added a note informing his readers that it was not made for the dead senior, but the living junior, Thomas Bissland. The same mansion, called Ferguslie House, now belongs to, and is occupied by, a gentleman whose initial is the next letter of the alphabet, a T. C., as benevolent and warm-hearted as ever was kind Tom of the Wood. Other portions of Ferguslie lands were purchased by Thomas Coats, Esq., at sundry times; and on 16th February, 1872, he acquired the estate of Ferguslie proper. Every person in Paisley, I am sure, wishes that gentleman long life and happiness to enjoy the lands of Ferguslie, rendered classic ground by Tannahill. The poet, on one occasion, while gazing in rapture at the grey-pinioned lark mounting to the skies in early morn, strung his lyre, and sung the following strain :—

Thomas Coats, Esq. of Ferguslie.

"Sweet Ferguslie, hail! thou'rt the dear sacred grove
  Where first my young muse spread her wing ;
Here Nature first waked me to rapture and love,
  And taught me her beauties to sing."

Granite memorial obelisk of Tannahill.

A granite monument has been erected over the grave of the Lyric Bard of Paisley, in the Cemetery of the former Relief Church, Canal-street, now called an United Presbyterian Church, bearing the following inscription :—

"TANNAHILL.

Born 3rd June, 1774.
Died 17th May, 1810.

Erected over the remains of the Poet, 1867."

Sad! sad! was the death of Tannahill, the author of the "Filial Vow;" who wrote these golden lines to his mother, then a widow—

"'Twas hers to guide me through life's early day,
To point out virtue's paths, and lead the way."[*]

Gloomy forebodings of mercantile complications had appeared at the close of the year 1810, and in February of the following year the extensive houses of Thomas Bissland & Company, merchants, Paisley; and Stuart, Locke, & Company, cotton spinners, Arthurlie, of which Thomas Bissland, junior, and William Stuart were partners, granted trust deeds for behoof of their creditors, in which they stated that they had lately, under the general distress in commercial affairs, become insolvent. William Stuart, besides Gryfe Castle, was owner of the large mansion, 55 High-street, Paisley, at the corner of Lady-lane, which he built in 1780, and also other properties throughout the town. Thomas Bissland afterwards became collector of customs in Greenock. William Stuart built a house in

Marginal note: Insolvencies in 1811.

---

[*] In the "Life of Tannahill," it is stated that he was the fourth child of his parents, James Tannahill, weaver, and Janet Pollock, who were married in 1762. He was, however, the fifth child. Their names, births, and baptisms appear in the register as follows:—

1st.	Robert,	born on	2nd August,	baptised, 2nd August,	1764
2nd.	Thomas,	„	27th November,	„ 3rd December,	1766
3rd.	Janet,	„	23rd April,	„ 23rd April,	1769
4th.	James,	„	17th September,	„ 19th September,	1771
5th.	Robert,	„	3rd June,	„ 5th June,	1774
6th.	Matthew,	„	14th July,	„ 17th July,	1777
7th.	Hugh,	„	25th January,	„ 25th January,	1780
8th.	Andrew,	„	19th March,	„ 19th March,	1784

Marginal note: Tannahill's brothers and sister.

Housebreaking and robbery at Gryffe Castle.

Garthland-place, Paisley, in 1819, and he died on 11th June, 1826.

The words " Gryffe Castle," already mentioned by me, bring to my recollection the crimes of housebreaking and robbery which occurred at the farm-house of that name, seventy-five years ago. On Sabbath evening, 19th March, 1797, between the hours of eleven and twelve o'clock, William Oak, weaver, Johnstone; Thomas Potts, weaver, Williamsburgh, Paisley; and William Pullans and George Aitcheson, weavers, Irvine, all Irishmen, broke into the house of John Barr, farmer, Gryffe Castle, Parish of Houston, armed with bludgeons, large knives, cutlasses, or swords. The female servant was the first to get up, and she acted the part of heroine on the occasion. The ruffians brandished their weapons over the heads of the inmates, threatening to take the life of Barr, and with horrid oaths and imprecations demanded money and the keys of the repositories. They robbed the house of £11 in notes, £1 in silver, and some silver spoons. The spoil was carried to Oak's house, and divided among the robbers. At that time John Barr had finished the building of a house in the Brig o' Weir, and had been up-lifting money from a bank in Paisley to pay the several tradesmen, but on that evening little money was in the house. The notorious Billy Oak was a strong, well-built man, fully six feet high, and about sixty years of age. Billy Oak came from Kilmarnock to Paisley about 1784, where he resided for ten years, chiefly in Bridge-street, *kept two wives*, and was a noted pugilist. He removed to the Brig o' Johnstone, where he resided three years, and occasionally travelled through the country with an ass or pony and cart, ostensibly hawking stone and earthenware. Potts had been previously charged with other crimes, and the large knife with which he was armed at the robbery was discovered concealed in a barrel about his premises. Potts and Aitcheson were both apprehended; but Aitcheson escaped from Irvine after his apprehension. Billy Oak and Billy Pullans both absconded, and a reward of £10 was offered for the apprehension of each of them. Aitcheson was again apprehended, and became a witness for the Crown. Both Oak and Potts were indicted to stand their trial before the High Court of Justiciary at Edinburgh, on Wednesday, 12th July, 1797. Oak was outlawed for not appearing, and the panel Potts pled "not guilty." The other Crown witnesses were John Barr and his wife, Janet M'Lellan, and their servants Jean Donaldson, James Rowan, and Joseph Lang. The exculpatory witnesses, whose testimony was merely on character, were John Brown, John Meikles's wife, Thomas Cochran, and Doctor Robinson. The jury found Potts guilty, and he was sentenced to be hanged at Paisley, on Thursday, 17th August, 1797. He wrote a long letter to his wife, Mary Potts, Williamsburgh, Paisley, dated Edinburgh, 14th July, 1797, which is now preserved in one of the cases of the Museum, Paisley. It is written on a sheet of foolscap paper, and the whole sheet is filled, with the exception of the place for the address. It is fairly written, without any trepidation, and is well composed; but there are a few defects in the spelling and capital letters of names. He gives a report of the trial, particularly his view of the examination of the witnesses. The female witnesses for the Crown were the weightiest against him, and he insinuates they were not in a state fit for examination, and that John Brown, one of his own witnesses, spoiled the case altogether in spontaneously referring to his (Potts's) previous imprisonment for other crimes. He says in the letter, " I am to be brought to paisley on monday

Trial of the robbers.

Thomas Potts sentenced to be hanged.

" the seventh day of agust, and to suffer on
" Thursday the seventeenth day of the same
" month, which I suppose is the fair day of

Erection of the
scaffold.

" paisley." The scaffold and gibbet for the execution were put up at the Cross of Paisley, where
the Jail was then situated, under the superintend-
ence of William Patison, Master of Works for the
Town. Two iron batts were fixed in the Cross
Steeple, at 17 and 26 feet from the ground, to
swing the gibbet, which was considered a very
simple and ingenious contrivance, so as to project
at the angle to be seen in Moss-street, the Cross,
and High-street. James Maxwell, poet in Paisley,
wrote a memorandum poem on the occasion, which

Poetical observa-
tions of Maxwell.

was printed, titled, "Observations on the awful
" execution of Thomas Potts, an Irishman, who
" was to be executed at the Cross of Paisley, upon
" Thursday, the seventeenth day of August, 1797,
" for housebreaking and robbery." In reference
to the number of persons concerned in the crimes,
the poet says—

" For out of four, but one is yet convicted,
    On whom just punishment can be inflicted ;
    For two are fled, and one a traitor turned,
    To get his just reward a while adjourned."

Execution of
Thomas Potts, 75
years ago.

The sentence of the High Court was carried into
execution on the day fixed, being in the week after
Saint James'-day Fair. Potts denied the crime
all along. During his confinement in Paisley Jail
after his condemnation, he was attended by all
the clergymen of the town, and at his particular
request was accompanied to the scaffold by the Rev.
Wm. Ferrier, of the Associate congregation. Potts
was interred opposite Shuttle-street in the Laigh
Church-yard. Sometimes a little levity is indulged
in, even on the occasion of a public execution ; and
John Parkhill, in his " Reminiscences of Paisley,
" personal and traditionary," annexed to his " Ten
" Years' Experience of a Betheral's Life," published

in 1859, relates one of these in reference to Potts's execution. Parkhill says that William Patison, the Master of Works, "met Rab Hamilton, and "told him in a very serious manner that he had "got a good job for him. 'Ay,' said Rab, "'What is that?' 'We are in great want o' a "hangman, and if thou likes to try thy han', "thou wilt be well paid for it.' 'Dit thysel',' said "Rab, 'thou's as keen o' siller as me.'" I have heard another version, and I will merely relate it, to show the dependence to be placed on oral tradition. The Master of Works, being very much satisfied with his own ingenuity in the construction of the gallows and new platform, was on the scaffold examining the efficiency of the workmanship; and on looking down to the crowd that was collected viewing the awful apparatus, he observed daft Rab Hamilton amongst them, and asked Rab to come up and try how it would fit; when Rab quickly responded, "Try it thysel', Will; "for thou's as cunning as me, and kens how to "work it." The Cross Steeple, built in the year 1757, was taken down in 1870, when the iron batts were taken out of the stones, and are now lying in the Museum, under the case containing the letter of Potts to his wife.

Gryffe Castle belonged, in 1797, to Mr. Houston of Jordanhill. John Barr, the tenant, was a member of the Reformed Presbyterian congregations at Kilmalcolm and Paisley, and attended the church in each of these places every alternate Sabbath. The house which Barr had finished in the Brig o' Weir in that or in the previous year, and had money about his domicile to pay the several tradesmen engaged upon the erection, now bears the *soubriquet* of "Dublin," from being inhabited chiefly by persons who had come from Ireland, in the beginning of the present century, for employment in the cotton mills of

The Master of Works and "Rab Hamilton."

the village. Joseph Lang, one of Barr's servants at the time of the robbery, and one of the witnesses at the trial, afterwards a blacksmith at the Brig o' Weir, is still living there, a hale, hearty old gentleman, ninety-two years of age. I called on him since I commenced my lectures. He was not aware of my coming, but I had a long conversation with him. His retentive memory is fresh and strong, and he related the circumstances attending the housebreaking and robbery as accurately and correctly as they are detailed in the prints of the period. I tested him on several points with general questions, and he answered them all specially and satisfactorily. There are very few persons who arrive at such an advanced age possessed of all their faculties. This nonogenarian, however, has all his senses in full activity, except that of hearing, as he suffers under a slight deafness. It was a perfect treat to enjoy his old reminiscences; and when it was proposed to bring his *specs* to enable him to sign his name to a judicial document, he at once resented the proposal, and wrote his name several times quickly and easily. Joseph's father was a blacksmith in the Brig o' Weir, Joseph himself was a blacksmith in the Brig o' Weir, and Joseph's son is a blacksmith in the Brig o' Weir, now a large village on the banks of the River Gryffe, in the parishes of Kilbarchan and Houston.

I may be permitted to refer to several of the tenants of the tenement of Miller and Bissland, erected in 1765 at the head of Saint Mirren's-street.

George Caldwell, weaver, the founder of the first circulating library in Paisley, became tenant of one of the shops. That intelligent weaver had, by his industry, acquired a considerable number of books, and his acquaintances proposed to him to form a lending library for the benefit of the inhabitants. He at once adopted the advice, and the desire for information proved successful. I believe it was that very library which gave the weavers of Paisley of that day a taste for literature, and raised them to be a very superior class of men, known far and wide for their information and intelligence. It is now a century since that humble library commenced ; and for fifty years young men climbed the face of the ladder of knowledge, and for the next fifty years they seemed to have been descending on the other side, when Sir Peter Coats came to the rescue, and founded the noble institution, the Free Public Library and Museum, for the instruction of the youth of the town in knowledge. The large building in which we are now assembled, with the entensive lending library, the magnificent reference library, the museum treasures, and this lecture hall, will be found an excellent school for young men of intelligence desirous of acquiring technical instruction. Mr. Caldwell drifted from being a lending librarian to being a bookseller, and removed to Moss-street, where he continued in business till he was the oldest bookseller in the West of Scotland. The late Provost Lumsden of Glasgow had his portrait taken and engraved.

At the division of the property, in 1771, the principal occupants were William Gilroy, baker ; Robert Pollock, grocer ; John Millar, one of the proprietors in the first flat ; Thomas Kibble, writer, in the second flat ; and Rev. George Muir, D.D., minister of the High Church, in the third flat. Dr. Muir was inducted in September, 1766, and died on 21st July, 1771, in the 48th year of his age and 21st of his ministry. In the Laigh churchyard there is a tombstone with the following inscription :— *Tenants at division of property.*

"Erected in memory of the Rev. George Muir, D.D., minister in Paisley. He was a faithful *Tombstone of Dr. Muir.*

minister, a loving husband, an affectionate parent, and agreeable companion. Beloved while he lived, he at his death left in the minds of his family, of his friends, and of his flock, a monument which time cannot destroy. He died the 21st of July, 1771, aged forty-seven. His wife, Isobel Wardlaw, died 2nd July, 1772, aged forty-eight."

Dr. Muir's sermons.

In 1771, a volume of his sermons were published with the following title page :—"The Parable of " the Tares, in 21 sermons ; by the Rev. Dr. " George Muir, late minister of the gospel in " Paisley. Printed by A. Weir and A. M'Lean. " Paisley, MDCCLXXI." These were the first printers in Paisley, and they commenced business in 1769.

William Gilroy, baker, had two brothers, Charles and John ; and he was succeeded by his brother Charles. In the Paisley department of the Glasgow Directory for 1783, the name of the latter will be found, —"Charles Gilroy, baker, Cross." Charles Gilroy, son of John, became an accountant and a commercial teacher ; and in the first Paisley Directory, published in 1810, his name appears, " C. Gilroy, accomptant, Abbey-

Second directory of Paisley.

close." In 1812 he published the second Directory of Paisley himself, and entered his own name, " C. Gilroy, teacher of writing and accounts, Cross." I exhibit one of his handbills, headed " C. Gilroy's mercantile academy, Cross, Paisley," which is also the frontispiece of his directory.

John Christie, soapmaker.

John Miller conveyed his portion of the property to Mary Miller, his eldest daughter, and John Christie, merchant in Smithhills of Paisley, her husband, and longest liver of them, in liferent, and their eldest son, John Christie, in fee, on 5th February, 1772 ; and they succeeded to it in 1791, on his death. John Christie introduced the soap manufacture into Paisley, and entered into partnership, in 1764, with John Dougal of

Easterhouse and John Burns of Lochridge. He was also a partner of the firm of Christie, Corse, & Muirhead, importers of timber; and the other partners were Robert Corse, of Greenlaw; Charles Addison, of Woodhead, Bo'ness; John Duguid, merchant, Glasgow; and Michael Muirhead, merchant there. They carried on an extensive trade with the coasts of the Baltic and Mediterranean, in which they employed their own ships. He was also the projector, and one of the ten original partners, of the Union Bank, Paisley, which commenced business in May, 1788. The other partners were George Houston, of Johnstone; John Semple, of Earnock; Charles Maxwell, of Merksworth; James Henderson, of Enochbank, Glasgow; Charles Addison, of Woodhead; John Cochran, Robert Hunter, Robert Orr, and John Christie, merchants in Paisley; and John Duguid, merchant in Glasgow. John Christie died shortly after his father-in-law, John Miller, as is seen from an additional inscription on the tombstone of the latter :—"John Christie died "14th Oct., 1791, aged 61 years; and Mary "Miller, spouse of John Christie, died 24th "Sept., 1826, aged 85 years."

John Christie, junior, merchant, Newtown, Paisley, executed on 9th January, 1794, a disposition in favour of Robert Corse, of Wester Greenlaw; William Stuart, merchant, Townhead (afterwards of Gryfe Castle before-mentioned); and Mary Miller or Christie, his mother; as trustees, for behoof of Elizabeth, Mary, George, Isobel, Agnes, Margaret, Janet, James, Jean, and Helen Christie, his brothers and sisters. John Christie, junior, died on 3rd April, 1827. George Christie was of an impulsive disposition, warmhearted, and very quick in temper. In the year 1803, when Napoleon threatened to invade the sea-girt isle, it is said that Paisley was the first

Margin notes:
Timber importers.

Union Bank of Paisley.

Christie family.

Volunteers in 1803.

James Christie.

town in Scotland to come forward with volunteers, and that George Christie was the first man enrolled, and consequently the first volunteer in Scotland. The Paisley regiment was also the first equipped and reviewed in Scotland. James Christie was born on 20th August, 1775. At his father's death, in 1791, he was assumed a partner in the soap - manufacturing business in New Sneddon-street, in place of his father. In July, 1808, when he retired from the soap-making firm, he went out to South America and commenced business along with George Cochran, at Rio de Janeiro, under the firm of Christie & Cochran. In 1814 he settled as a merchant in Glasgow, and in executing his commercial transactions he had occasion to visit many places on the Continent of Europe, which greatly improved his fund of information, and made him good company in meetings of his friends. He was brother-in-law to David Prentice, editor of the *Glasgow Chronicle,* a paper of very advanced Liberal opinions. Mr. Christie took an active interest in the local politics of the neighbouring city, and firmly maintained the principles so long ably advocated in the *Chronicle* newspaper. In 1827, Mr. James Christie purchased all the properties on the north side of High-street between the Coffee-Room and Paisley Bridge, commonly called the Old Bridge, and took down the houses that had been erected thereon after the great fire of 1733. On the site he erected substantial and most expensive buildings, consisting of shops, offices, and dwelling-houses. On the side fronting the river Cart he constructed a terrace, below which was formed a tavern, well-known as the Terrace Tavern. The whole were called Christie-buildings and Christie-terrace. However much the town was adorned by these expensive buildings, it was an unfortunate speculation for Mr. Christie,

Christie buildings.

and sadly reduced the comforts of himself and his family. The Christies feued a field of Wester Crossflat for building, in which were formed two short streets, and they called the one leading off Glasgow-road "Christie-street," for the father; and the other, running off Mill-street, after their mother, "Miller-street."

The tombstone of Mr. Miller and Mr. Christie, before noticed, was superseded by the erection of three new tombstones, the one in the centre to the memory of Mr. Miller and his wife and Mr. Christie and his wife; the one on the right to the memory of James Christie, his wife, and daughter; and the other, on the left, to the memory of other members of the Christie family :—

(Centre Stone.)
To the most holy and Triune God
Be Glory for ever. Amen.
Beneath are deposited the mortal
Remains of JOHN MILLER of Dykes,
Sometime Merchant in Paisley,
Born 1711, Died 5th May, 1791;
And of Mrs. ELIZABETH CRAIG, his wife,
Born 1713, Died 11th September, 1779;
And of their Son-in-law,
JOHN CHRISTIE, Merchant in Paisley,
Owner of the lands of Greenhill,
Wester Crosslet, and others,
Born at Idenmill, Aberdeenshire,
4th February, 1730, and Died in
Newtown of Paisley, 11th October, 1791;
And of Mrs. MARY MILLER, his Widow,
Born at Grangehill, Beith, 13th June, 1741,
and Died in Newtown, Paisley,
24th September, 1826;
and also of
JAMES CHRISTIE, late Merchant
in Glasgow, son of the last and
Grandson of the first named,
Born at Paisley, 20th August, 1775,
And Died at Oakfield Place, Glasgow,
On Ash Wednesday, 1852.
(Christie Arms.) *

Tombstone of
John Miller,

John Christie,

and

James Christie.

---

* The dates, 11th September and 11th October, were 14th September and 14th October on the old stone. The discrepancies are engraver's errors

Tombstone of James Christie.

(Stone on the right side.)
D . O . M .
In Pious Memory of
JAMES CHRISTIE,
Late Merchant in Glasgow,
Born at Paisley, 1775,
Died at Glasgow, 1852 ;
And of his Widow,
Mrs. MARY CRAIG,
Born at Nantwick, 1783,
Died at Bedley, 1857 ;
And of their Daughter-in-law,
Mrs. CATHERINE CAMERON CAMPBELL,
of Bedley and Petershill,
Born at Petershill, 1820,
Died at Bedley, 1854.
Their remains were removed from this place to the
new vault at Bedley, 14th December, 1857.

———

Tombstone of Christie family.

(Stone on the left side.)
Here lies interred,
ELIZABETH,
Born 1763, Died 1844 ;
MARY,
Born 1767, Died 1847 ;
AGNES,
Born 1770, Died 1848 ;
MARGARET,
Born 1771, Died 1829,
Daughters of the Deceased
JOHN CHRISTIE, Esq.,
Merchant, Paisley.
Here also lies interred
GEORGE CHRISTIE,
his son,
Sometime Merchant, Paisley,
Born 1776, Died 1844.

Tombstone of William Miller in Kilmaurs.

It will be observed that the death of the eldest
son, John Christie, jun., is not mentioned. On
the tombstone of William Miller of Dykes, great-
grandfather of the Christies, who died 12th Oct.,
1753, erected to his memory in Kilmaurs Kirkyard, there is inscribed the following lines :—

" Though tombs prove faithless to their trust,
    And bodies moulder into dust,
    A good man's name shall ever last,
    In spite of every nipping blast."

I have given the three inscriptions in the Abbey cemetery of the Millers and Christies, as specimens of full and chaste mortuary literature. The generality of those in Paisley Cemetery have become so poor and meagre, that an improvement is absolutely necessary. The inscription on a monument is the true memorial of the deceased; and what is called the monument is for the sculptor. The visitor converses with the inscription, and only takes a passing glance at the sculptor's monument. Lettering is twenty times less expensive than ornamental embellishments; and I trust inscriptions in future will be more worthy of holding converse with visitors. From the numerous texts of Scripture now engraved by sculptors on the bases of monuments, strangers will be apt to conclude that there are no publicans and sinners in Paisley.

Robert Bennett, grocer in Paisley, acquired from Thomas Bissland, sometime wright and merchant, then in the Newtown of Paisley, the eastmost house and shop, occupied by him, at the price of £412, on the 28th of January, 1800. Mr. Bennet came from Borrowstouness, and he dealt largely in salt manufactured in that place. He called his shop the "Bo'ness salt office," which was well patronised for that necessary article of domestic consumpt. Bo'ness was a celebrated place for making salt, and the manufacture had been carried on there for the preceding 500 years. I have already alluded to several tenants in the upper part of the large tenement, and I will now notice another tenant who began business in the basement storey, below the salt office, about the beginning of the present century, under the sign of "The Last," with the following distich,—

"I have travelled all day to find good Ale,
    And at the Last I found it."

Joseph Howell, the tenant, was an Englishman;

s

and having obtained encouragement in his business, he extended his accommodation to the back
land of the premises, to carry on the trade of a
restaurant. He prepared a handbill for the information of the public, which was handed to
old John Neilson to print; and, being written
phonetically in representation of the provincial
style of speaking in the district to which Howell
belonged, Neilson printed the handbill *literatim*
as follows :—

JOSEPH HOWELL hed of the waterwind oposit the
keall markit onst more returns is great full thanks
to the ledis and gentlemen of paisley and nebrood
for thar kind incurigment hee like wis in forms the
gentlemen of paisley that hee as got a privet rume
a bove is ^one^ kichin where hee in tends to meake
redy thrue the sumer Beef steks the refind sosegs
and minsed Colops evry day evry strict a tenshon
will bee given to all horders the ^famylise^ might de-
pend on the best quolity of meat anand the strict
ist clanlyness Brad the flesher to prevent hoing Complaints of drysosegs or stell meet he byse is ^fresh^ meat
every day Cuts no more down then is reglar
sel will a lowofas the famylise may have jt
in reall perfection the re refind sosegs as bene a
proved of by Paisley gentellmen and gentlemen and
sum gentle men from glashoo and hedenbrogh and
london and for ^i^ n gentlemen to bee the furst sosegs
that herr was henterdust for seele orders from the
toun and from the cuntry will bee greatefull receved
and b- punctall exicuted.

Paisley, 15th June, 1803.   J. Neilson, Printer.

The handbill excited considerable laughter among
the intelligent Paisley bodies, proving, as it did,
that a clever, tidy Englishman could not write the
King's English. But Joseph's good cookery and
his bad orthography had the desired effect of drawing customers under "The Last." At another time

he had a sign of himself, at the noble occupation

of carving a joint of meat, with the following distich underneath :—

"Good meat and drink make men to grow,
   And you will find it just below."

In the first Paisley Directory, published for the year 1810, he is entered "Joseph Howell, vintner, St. Mirren's-street;" and in the second Directory of 1812, prepared by Charles Gilroy, he is entered "Joseph Howell, beef-steak, sausage, and oyster tavern, Cross," he having removed to the Plainstanes.—Robert Bennett was succeeded in 1817 by his son, John Bennett, writer in Hamilton; and he, again, was succeeded in 1847 by his cousin, once removed, David Barley, forester, Borrowstouness. He sold the premises to Mrs. Mary Miller or M'Donald, wife of David M'Donald, mentioned in the first lecture, on 30th June, 1853, for £255.

Thomas Bissland sold the flat above the shops of Robert Bennett and Robert Pollock to George Murdoch, merchant in Paisley, on 8th November, 1799. He was a cloth merchant at the end of the Old Bridge. His daughter Jessie was married to Colonel Charles Downie, of the Spanish service, mentioned in the second lecture.

George Murdoch, on 24th April, 1818, conveyed the flat to Messrs. Neil M'Donald and James Dunn, and they carried on business therein as manufacturers, under the firm of M'Donald & Dunn. The company was dissolved in 1824, and Mr. Dunn conveyed his half to Mr. M'Donald, on 26th July, 1824. Mr. M'Donald built a house in Love-street, in 1817, which he called *Seeding Hall*, from the fancy fabric (with the figures of seeds thereon) which he manufactured, and from the sale of which he had made his money. The house now belongs to the Middle Church congregation, and is called the Middle Parish

George Murdoch.

M'Donald and Dunn.

Seeding Hall.

The Greenhill.

Manse, presently occupied by the Rev. Robert Duncan. Mr. M'Donald was elected Town Treasurer in 1823, and Bailie in 1824 and 1825. Mr. Dunn, in 1825, built a mansion on the apex of the Greenhill, in Underwood-street, which he called, and which has been known since as, Greenhill House. He had an excellent taste for design, and his patterns for sewed muslins were highly esteemed in the market; and in laying off the grounds at Greenhill he displayed the same fine taste there. He died on 26th February, 1870, in the 79th year of his age. The Greenhill is a small mount about 16 feet higher than the surrounding land, and very probably received the name from its verdure of green. It would be a beautiful spot in olden times, in the midst of the barren dreary waste, being bounded on the east and south by the Common, covered with indigenous wild moorland plants and shrubs; on the west, by the marsh of Finnies-bog, the habitat of frogs and toads; and on the north, by the black moss of Paisley, covered with heather and cotton grass. From the oldest volume of the Town Council Records now extant, it appears that the good ground of the "Greinhill" had been subdivided among the Burgesses, previous to 1594. It will be seen from the inscription on John Christie's tombstone that Greenhill belonged to him at his decease. Greenhill was next acquired by John Love, of the Hope Temple, and next by Mr. Dunn.—David M'Donald, whom I have already noticed, succeeded his father, and in 1855 disponed the flat to his wife, Mary Miller or M'Donald.

James Tait and his several properties.

Thomas Bissland disponed the third flat to James Tait, manufacturer, Paisley. In the year 1808, Mr. Tait built the large three-storey house, No. 9 Moss-street, to carry on his business; and the same year, he erected the large four-storey house, No. 101 High-street, next to the Town's

House, or Saracen's Head Inn. By erecting these houses he built beyond his means, like many more individuals, and became bankrupt on 16th October, 1810. Both of these properties were sold in separate shops and separate flats, to realise better prices out of them. The latter house, built by Mr. Tait, has now become a great obstruction to the immediate improvement of the High-street, from its value, and there being six proprietors to treat with. The removal of the falling Cross steeple allowed the projected improvement of the High-street to commence at the right place ; and since it has been carried so far as 65 feet, every candid person now admits that the benefit of widening the street at that dangerous place far surpasses the advantage to be derived from retaining an old tottering steeple.

The Trustees of Mr. Tait sold the flat to Mr. Robert Farquharson, manufacturer, Paisley, and his wife, Mrs. Jane Nairne, in 1816, and longest liver of them. Mr. Farquharson was the son of the Rev. Robert Farquharson of Allargue, minister of Logie Coldstone, in the county of Aberdeen. Mrs. Farquharson was a daughter of Alexander Nairne, soap merchant, the gentleman who erected the fine old Mansion House on the lands of the Brabloch, Renfrew-road, about the year 1800. Robert Farquharson came to Paisley in 1801, and was admittted a Burgess of the Burgh in 1805. He was the chief partner in the firm of Robert Farquharson & Co., manufacturers, who commenced business in Moss-street, and removed to the above flat when it was purchased ; and their names are entered in the Directory for 1810. Mr. Farquharson was elected a Bailie in 1819 and 1821, and Provost in 1824, 1825, and 1826. In private life he was a warm-hearted friend ; in business, an upright and respectable gentleman ; in civic matters, execut-

Provost Robert Farquharson.

Distress of 1826.

Presentation of Plate.

Dinner to Provost Farquharson.

ing his duties honestly and fearlessly ; in politics, of high Tory principles. During his civic reign, one of the most appalling periods of distress occurred that ever visited Paisley, and continued for a whole year. Thousands of the population could not obtain employment, and were without the means of support. The Provost then showed himself the right man in the right place for the friendless and distressed, and, assisted by committees, he and they put their shoulders to the wheel, and by unwearied exertions met all the difficulties without a murmur. When the dark black cloud of distress that had hung over the town for such a length of time, had passed away, the people recognised the valuable services of the worthy Provost, and presented him, at a public meeting held in the Saracen's Head Inn, on 31st September, 1827, presided over by Mr. William Craig, surgeon, with three beautiful and chastely-designed silver salvers, subscribed for by fifteen hundred working men, and bearing the following inscription :—" To Robert Farquharson, Esq. of " Allargue, Provost of Paisley, as an expression " of public gratitude for his exertions in behalf of " the unemployed operatives during the late " period of unexampled distress." The Provost, afterwards, notwithstanding his politics being in a minority in Paisley, was so much respected by the inhabitants, that it would have been almost a crime to breathe a word against his fair name and fame. In 1859, Provost Farquharson succeeded to the entailed estate of Breda, in the parish of Alford, Aberdeenshire ; and before he left town to return to his native place, 750 of his townsmen entertained him at dinner on Thursday, 25th June, 1857. Provost Brown presided on the occasion, and three ex-Provosts acted as croupiers. Provost Farquharson died in the 81st year of his age. A monumental stone has been erected in the cemetery of Alford to his memory, bearing the following inscription :—" Erected by his " Widow, in affectionate remembrance of Robert " Farquharson of Allargue and Breda, born the " 13th of January, 1783, died the 14th of February, " 1863." In a few years thereafter another monument was erected in the same place, bearing the following inscription :—" Erected by her daugh- " ters, in memory of their loved mother, Jean " Nairne Farquharson, widow of the late Robert " Farquharson of Allargue and Breda, who died " on the 14th April, 1870, in her 81st year, at " Breda." In looking over the list of gentlemen who have filled the civic chair in Paisley, I observe several had arrived at that dignity in their adopted town ; and, in taking a glance at other places, I find they are indebted to natives of Paisley for the discharge of similar duties. I may instance James Watson, Esq., the present Lord Provost of the city of Glasgow, who was born and educated in Paisley.

Mrs. Farquharson, the surviving owner of the third flat, and Walter M'Kenzie, Esq., accountant in Glasgow, trustee on the sequestrated estate of David M'Donald, owner of the remainder of the property, entered into an arrangement to dispose of the whole in one lot; and they exposed the subjects to public roup, on 24th May, 1866, at the upset sum of £1500, when the Commissioners of Police became the purchasers at that price.

The elevation of the edifice on the property bears ample evidence of the genius of the architect who planned the five-storey house, and the ability of the two merchant princes who proceeded with an erection so far in advance of the age. The pilaster columns, rustic angles, and window architraves, at once proclaim the conception of that eminent architect, Bailie John Whyte, stamp-master, Paisley, who planned this

Architect of the large tenement.

specimen erection for future modern buildings in
Paisley. The house measures 40 feet in front,
and 57 feet high from the basement to the
chimney top. The height from the floor to ceil-
ings are,—basement storey, six feet; the ground
or shop flat, eight feet; the next two flats, each
nine feet; and the upper flat, eight feet nine
inches. There are five windows in front of each
of the three upper flats, two dormer windows in
the attics, and a skylight in the cock-loft. Altogether, the house has a proportionable appearance,
and such as would be expected from the artistic
hands of a gentleman who had obtained a reputa-
tion for laying off elegant mansions and planning
handsome steeples.*

Sale of the old materials.

Pulling down the tenement.

* On the 28th of May, 1872, James R. M'Fadyen, auctioneer,
advertised that he was instructed by the Commissioners of
Police to sell the whole of the old materials of Nos. 13 and 14
Saint Mirren's-street and 116 Causeyside. On Wednesday, 5th
June following, he rouped all the materials of these houses,
which realised £216. Several of the tenants removed their
effects when the roup began, and the sale was scarcely concluded when the fortunate purchasers commenced taking
down the well-finished doors, shutters, and wainscoting, that
had been carefully fitted up above a hundred years before.
Peter Wallace, wright, purchaser of the stone work, commenced on 11th June to take down the east chimney top. On
Wednesday evening following, the 13th, the stone stair, joist-
ing, and flooring of all the flats fell down with a crash to the
bottom, and enveloped the Cross in a dense cloud of dust.
The following morning, a large squad of the workmen of Mr.
William Gillespie, at considerable peril, commenced pulling
down, with ropes and other appliances, the dangerous building, which was full of cracks and had no band,—the mortar
being thoroughly rotten. During the dinner hour a large
portion of the back wall fell to the ground. The men wrought
vigorously, sometimes in imminent danger, and had the
whole walls levelled by Saturday. Large crowds visited the
scene of demolishing the first-class and highest house built
in Paisley in the year 1765.

END OF THIRD LECTURE.

IV.

The Paslay Tak,

Now, No. 6 High Street.

—

HIS is the fourth and last lecture on the "Old Places," and relates to the tenement which was called *Paslay Tak*, the feu of which was granted by Abbot Robert Schaw to Richard Brigton, on 21st April, 1500,—the last year of the fifteenth century. I will commence, as formerly, with giving the principal parts of the Charter :—

"*Carta Ricardi Brigtoune*

"*Ombs hac carta visuris et audituris Robts pmissione abbas mostij de paslet convtos eiusd ordis cluniacens glas dios Stm in dno Noveris vnversi pntes et faci nos dctos abbas ac convtu capli vnam pmsis vtilitat concen et assen nri mostij congregati dedisse concisse et p pnti carta nras assedasse et ad firma dimissise delecto scutari nro Ricardo brigtoune p eius bono servio nob a pdecessori nro als mltptem facte Totm et integrm illud nrm tenemtu qd vocar paslay tak Jacen in brgo nro de paslay ex pte austli Regij vici eius situat in aglo int tenetu andre pator vocatu le vnhouss ex pt austli et tenetu david alexr pt occideli et com via regia ex boreali et orientali ptbus Quod qd tenetu continen in frot ateriori ex pt boreali nonem vlnas et qtua vnus vlne et in fronte anteriori ex pt orientali octo vlnas sup pub viciis regii ptibus In cuj rej testiom sigillm cm capti nri vna concensu euisd ptbus et appesu Apd nrm mostim aut dtm xxi die mesis aplis ao dmo millio quin gentesimo.*

TRANSLATION.

"CHARTER OF RICHARD BRIGTON.

"To all who shall see and hear this Charter, Robert,

T

Charter of
Richard Brigton.

21st April, 1500.

Translation of
Charter.

by permission, Abbot of the Monastery of Paslay, and convent there, of the order of Cluny, in the diocese of Glasgow, Greeting in the Lord, Be it known to all present and to come, we, the said Abbot and Convent, chapterally assembled, with one consent and assent, in the premises, and for the utility of our said Monastery, have given, granted, and by this our present charter assigned, and in feu farm dimitted, to our beloved buckler, Richard Brigton, for his many good services rendered to us, and also to our predecessors, All and Whole that our tenement, which is called Paslay Tak, lying in our Burgh of Paslay, on the south part of the king's high street thereof, situated in the angle between the tenement of Andrew Pantor, called the Un-houss, on the south, and the tenement of David Alexander on the west part, and the king's common high street on the north and east parts; which tenement contains in the fore front, on the north part, nine and one-fourth part ells, and in the fore front on the east part, eight ells, upon the public street and other parts : In witness whereof, our common seal with one consent of our chapter there, is hung to these presents, at our Monastery foresaid, xxi day of the month of April, in the year of our Lord one thousand five hundred."

Richard Brigton's other Charters.

The first appearance of Richard Brigton was his obtaining a charter from Abbot George Schaw, on 16th May, 1490, of a piece of ground lying upon the water of Kert, and bounded by the Common Passage, near the water of Kert, on the east. From that description, it would seem that the Common Passage, in continuation of the passage commonly called the "Hole o' the Wa'," ran along the river side, from the Wattirgait northward. That district was then the inferior part of the town, and the erections in that quarter were bothies of the most primitive description. Richard Brigton at the same time obtained another Charter, dated the same day, 16th May,

1490, of a piece of outfield land lying in the Regality of Paisley, and within the Sheriffdom of Renfrew, containing one acre, with eight falls, between the wood of Darskaith on the east, and the lands of Ferguslie on the west. That piece of ground was afterwards called Serjeant's Acre, and I suppose it acquired that name from the official situation held by Richard. That piece of ground was afterwards acquired by the Lairds of Ferguslie, and it has always been, since the date of acquirement, conveyed by the original and separate description from the lands of Ferguslie, and now belongs to Thomas Coats, Esq. of Ferguslie, and lies on the east side of his mansion-house. Richard Brigton also obtained a Charter, on 10th September, 1498, of a tenement, bounded by the tenement of Andrew Pantor on the south, and the tenement of David Alexander on the west.

Serjeant's Acre.

On 28th December, 1504, a summons from the Lords of Council, at the instance of a venerable father in Christ, Robert, Abbot of our Monastery of Paisley, and religious men of the Convent there, against John Lord Ross of Halkhed, and others, for unjustly entering upon, and occupying, the lands of Thornle, without permission, was addressed by King James IV. to Sir Henry Schaw of Gartuly, Richard Schaw of Crago, Henry Carns, George Crawfurd, Allan Stewart, Robert Smyth, *Richard Brigton,* John Brown, and Robert Smyth, and each of them conjunctly and severally, his sheriffs in that part, Greeting, and commanding them to execute the summons. George Crawfurd served the summons on 7th January, 1504, personally, on the defenders.

Action of ejection : Abbot Robert Schaw against John, Second Lord Ross.

The tenement under consideration was called the "PASLAY TAK," but there is no indication in the charter whatever of the meaning of these words. The word "*Tak*" may mean a lease, or the place

The meaning of the word Tak.

to *tak* customs, or *tak* poinds for unpaid customs.
I am inclined to attach the latter meaning to
the word, and to think that Richard Brigton
had been the collector of customs,—a tak or tax-
gatherer, or serjeant of the regality of the Monastery, a King's messenger or sheriff in that part,
previous to obtaining the feu of the Paslay Tak.
The tenement stood at the market-place of Paisley,
where all the markets and fairs of the Burgh were
originally held, for buying and selling all kinds
of merchandise.

Situation of the Market Cross of Paisley.

The Charter of King James IV., erecting the village of Paslay into a Burgh of Barony, on 19th August, 1488, allowed the Burgesses and inhabitants
to possess a cross and market-place for ever, every
week, on Monday, and two public fairs yearly
(one on the day of Saint Mirin, and the other on
the day of Saint Marnock), with tolls and other
liberties pertaining to fairs.   The cross was accordingly erected in front of the property now
No. 8 High-street, presently belonging to Messrs.
Robert Barr and William Wotherspoon.   The
cross was so situated that persons coming to the
market-place from the east, up the Smiddie-hills
and over the Bridge, could see it; those coming
from the west country, down the King's common
highway, would see it; and those coming from
the north, up Moss-street, should see it.   The
Bailies of the Royal Burgh of Renfrew considered
they had a right to levy all the customs in the
Barony of Renfrew, and that the *takyn* of the
customs by the Burgh of Paisley was an invasion of
their ancient rights; and they sent their officers
to Paisley to *tak* the customs.   On their arrival

Dinging down the Cross by the lawless officers of Renfrew.

at the market-place, they " violently dang doun
" the cross, and forcibly seised a quarter of beef
" for a pennie of custom, ane cabock of cheyss for
" a halfpennie of custom, and a wind of quhit
" claith for a pennie of custome,"—beef, cheese,

and white cloth being the articles for sale that day in the market. Bailie John Whiteford, the first Bailie of Paisley (the lineal descendant of Walter de Whiteford, one of the victors at the battle of the Largs, who fought against the Norwegians in 1263) and his Burgesses of Paisley, instantly vindicated the rights and privileges of the then new Burgh by retaking the beef, cheese, and cloth from the band of lawless officers and their accomplices from Renfrew. This was the first conflict between the two Burghs; and if tradition is correct, the animosity has been continued till a very recent date. In 1491, the Bailies, burgesses, and community of Renfrew raised an action before the Lords of Parliament, against John Whitefurd, Bailie to the Abbot of Paslay, "for "wrangous spoliation and takin fra the officers of "Renfrew of certain poynds they had taken for "custom, and concluding for restitution." The Abbot appeared in the case with his Bailie; and parties being heard, and their Charters produced and read, the Lords Auditors found the said Bailie "had done na fraud, nor usurpet apoun "the privileg of the Burgh of Renfrew, in takin "fra the officers of the said Burgh of the said "poinds; because the said town and lands of "Paslay were create in ane fre barony and "regality, proved by a Charter under King "Robert's grate sele, of the date precedand the "infeftment maid to the said town of Renfrew." That finding or decree was confirmed by Parliament on 22nd June, 1493. In December, 1495, George Schaw, Abbot of Paisley, raised an action against the Bailies and Community of the Burgh of Renfrew, "for the wrangous takin the customs "within the regalitie and barony of Paslay for "100 years, and also for the wrangous destruction "and castene doune of ane market cros of that "toun of Paslay." The damage done to the cross

Vindication by Bailie Whiteford and his burgesses.

Decree against Burgh of Renfrew for violent seizure.

Action of Abbot Schaw against Burgh of Renfrew.

was estimated by the Abbot at six merks. The Abbot also concluded for other claims of damages for more invasions of their rights and privileges.

Charter to the tenement at the Cross.

In July, 1517, Abbot Robert Schaw sealed a Charter to Nicholas Stewart, his well-beloved familiar servant, of a " burgal tenement that was "formerly Walter Strathy's, lying in the south "part of the said Burgh, in the *great street near* " *the 'cross' of the market-place.*" From that description, and the boundaries of Stewart's tenement, which is now the property No. 8 High-street, the market cross would be erected opposite the window of Mr. Robert Barr, druggist, in the present building. The breadth of the street or area of the market-place was certainly entitled to be called the "great street," compared with the other narrow passages of the Burgh. The situation of the cross is here distinctly pointed out, and that is the only Charter in which it was mentioned. In the Rental of the Altars within the Parish Kirk of Paisley, the altar dedicated to Saint James and Saint Nicolas has xiijs iiijd yearly from the " The

House forenent,

or

besouth the Cross.

"houss foirnent the corss, on the south syde of "the gait, now perteining to robt montgomerie of "Skelmorlie." The property is again entered in the Pittance Rental as " ye tenement besouth the " corss, perteining to Robt. Montgomerie of Skel-"morlie, and pays 13s. 4d. yearly." His father, Robert Montgomerie of Skelmorlie, and his elder brother, William Montgomerie, were the persons

Murder of the two Montgomeries.

who were both murdered by the Maxwells of Newark, on 3rd July, 1584, which finished the great feud of a hundred years between the Montgomeries and Sempills on the one side, and the Cunninghams and Maxwells on the other side. Exactly two hundred years after the officers of the Burgh of Renfrew had " castene doun the cross," the Town Council of Paisley concluded that the cross should be removed, and the place where it stood calsyed. It is not stated whether the removal in 1693 took place from Presbyterian zeal, or from the cross interrupting the traffic of the street.

Removal of the Cross

The market-place of Paisley is 178 feet long from east to west, 74 feet in breadth at the east end, and 50 feet at the west end. All kinds of goods and merchandise were exposed for sale there, and the principal articles sold in olden times were meal, fish, flesh, cheese, eggs, butter, salt, lint, wool, linen, cloth, and shoes. About 1665, the bulky articles of meal and beef required more accommodation, and meal and flesh markets were separately erected. The meal market was built on the property now No. 26 High-street (presently belonging to Mr. John Gibb); and the armorial stone, with coat of arms used at that time, which was in the front wall, is deposited in the Museum. The flesh market was erected on the property No. 5 Moss-street; afterwards removed, in 1767, to the opposite side of the street, where the Exchange Buildings are now situated. The green market was on the north side of the area; and, in 1777, a portion of that side, measuring 72 feet in length and 22 feet in breadth, was pavemented and enclosed with 18 stone palls. It was the place where merchants and Bailies most did congregate, and was vulgarly called the "*Plain Stanes.*" Shortly after the passing of the Paisley Police Act of 1806, the Commissioners of Police reduced the breadth of the " plain stanes " to seven feet, the maximum breadth of pavement fixed by the statute, and causewayed the 15 feet thus thrown into the street. In 1865, the new Commissioners of Police, appointed in 1864 under the General Police Act for 1862, increased the breadth of the pavement three feet,—making its breadth now ten feet.

Market-place at the Cross.

Meal market.

Flesh market.

The Plain Stanes.

Market days.

The market days were originally fixed for Monday by the Charter of Erection of the Burgh. The day was afterwards changed to Friday; and I find that in 1648, in the time of the Commonwealth, sermon was appointed on Friday, being the market day. On the Town Council obtaining their Charter from King Charles II., on 8th December, 1665, Friday was appointed the market-day. In thirty years afterwards, on 28th January, 1697, the Town Council, considering that Beith market day was also held on Friday, which was injurious to both markets, altered the market day of Paisley to Thursday, and it has continued on Thursday till the present time. Beith market day has continued on Friday till the present period.

Paisley fairs of Saint Mirin and Saint Marnock.

The fairs appointed to be held by the Charter of Erection of the Burgh, were Saint Mirin's day and Saint Marnock's day,—the former was held on 15th September, and the latter on 25th October. I have already shown that one Calendar of Scots Saints adopted the 15th, and another adopted the 17th September. The Calender of Saints gave 25th October, and Professor Cosmo Innes gives 25th November, as Saint Marnock's day. The Town Council afterwards substituted Saint James's day, 25th July, for the fair on Saint Mirin's day. In the Charter of 1665, two public fairs were appointed to be held yearly,—one on 26th June, commonly called Saint James the Apostle's day, and the other on

Saint James and Saint Marnock Fairs.

26th October, commonly called Saint Marnock's day. Saints' days, it would seem, were not very well known by the Merry Monarch and his Government, because they had committed an error of a month with the former, and a day with the latter. Fairs were the chief terms for transacting business in olden times; and the Town Council having applied to Parliament for two additional fairs, an Act was passed on 4th August, 1690, granting other two fairs,—one to be held on the first Thursday of February, and the other on the first Tuesday of May, annually. All these fair days were altered by the Town Council about 150 years ago, to the third Thursday of February, called Candlemas fair; the third Thursday of May, called Beltan or Whitsunday fair; the second Thursday of August, called Saint James-day fair; and the second Thursday of November, called Martinmas fair. In 1815, the Town Council obtained another Crown Charter for political purposes, which also contained authority to hold two fairs,—viz., one on the 25th day of July, called James the Apostle's day, and the other on the 25th day of October, called Saint Marnock's day, yearly. This latter Charter, although it gave the correct festival days of the two saints, was never acted on so far as the fair days themselves were concerned.

Paisley fairs were celebrated markets in olden times, and very much frequented by dealers in horses and cattle, tradesmen with articles of utility, packmen with their merchandise, bagpipers, ballad-singers, and a long list of attendants and mendicants, all endeavouring to turn a penny. The rural population from the country parishes of the county and neighbouring shires, flocked to the fair to make their purchases, and to enjoy a general holiday. The horse-race instituted in 1620 by the Town Council of Paisley, called the "Bell Race," from their presenting "Silver Bells," to be run for annually, was an attraction for drawing crowds of people to the fair. These fairs and races have both been celebrated in song and elegy. In a song, ascribed to John, Duke of Argyll, titled, "Argyll is my name," there is the following verse respecting the fair,—

"I'll buy a fine present to bring to my dear,
A pair of fine garters for Maggie to wear,

Marginal notes:
Candlemas, Whitsunday, Saint James, and Martinmas Fairs.

Paisley Fairs.

Horse Race for Silver Bells.

Argyll is my name.

And some pretty things else, I do declare,
When she gangs wi' me to Paisley fair."

And Robert Sempill, one of the Beltrees poets, in his "Elegy on Habbie Simson," the piper of Kilbarchan, has a verse on the races,—

" And at horse races many a day,
Before the black, the brown, the gray,
He gart his pipe, when he did play,
   Baith skirl and skreid ;
Now all such pastime's quite away
   Sen' Habbie's deid."

On 9th February, 1529, Abbot John Hamilton granted to James Foster, Burgess of Paisley, a Charter of the same subjects, called "Paslay Tak." On 11th February, 1541, Henry Baxter, Claustral Prior of the Monastery of Paisley, and commissioner for Abbot John Hamilton in his absence, granted a Charter to John Dowhill, Burgess of Paisley. The Abbot at that time was in France, and during his absence the Claustral Prior sealed twelve Charters to vassals. On the accession of the infant Queen Mary, of six days of age, to the throne of Scotland, on 13th December, 1542, disputes arose respecting the Regency of the kingdom. The Earl of Arran wrote for

his brother, the Abbot, to return. Ralph Sadler, the English ambassador to Scotland, considering it an important event, mentioned it in a letter to King Henry VIII., on 31st July, 1543. King Henry VIII., however, was aware of the importance of conciliating the brother of Arran, and he

entertained the Abbot on his passing through London, on his way to Paisley. Patrick Tytler, in his "History of Scotland," in noticing that circumstance, and referring to Sadler as his authority, said, "Hamilton, an Abbot of Paisley, " the natural brother of the Governor, and an " ecclesiastic of considerable political ability, had

" returned from France." The first Charter granted by Abbot Hamilton after his return from France was on 11th August, 1543, to John Wilson, of the lands of *Castleheid.*

The hiatus of a hundred years occurring in the history of Paisley properties, referred to in the first lecture, now takes place, and I may fill it up with a brief description of the town in 1560. The population would not exceed 700 persons, who would require 180 dwellings for their accommodation. With a few exceptions, such as Thomas Inglis's house at the Brig-end, Lord Sempill's heyt house (formerly called the Chamberlain's House) at the corner of Saint Mirin's-wynd, the Heyt house or Common Hall at the market-place, (marked No. 2 on the plan), Sir John Wan's Lady Priest's house, and William Sempill's of Third Part, both in the High-street,—all the other houses were of the most original and primitive description,—mere huts, built with the readiest stones and clay at hand. The roofs were covered with heather and turves, plenty of which could be found in the common of Broomlands, or moss of Paisley. There was only one dwelling-house per acre of ground, from the West Port to the Vennel ; and as the town increased, these acres were sold in halves, and again subdivided into roods, as appears from the front of the steadings at the present day. These, however, are not uniform, some being larger and others smaller, arising from the manner in which the original owner erected the first house. If he occupied a large front, he left a small gap to be afterwards filled and built up. Moss-Raw, Wattirgait, and the passage along the banks of the Kert, were the inferior parts of the town, and the buildings there were boothies, occupied by the lower class of society. The streets of the Burgh were mere surface roadways, used for horse traffic, and in

Marginal notes:

Gap in the history of Paisley.

Appearance of buildings.

Streets.

Oldest building.

Fulzie heaps.

wet weather must have been a puddle of mud. The streets, or rather grass roads, were also used for collecting the fulzie of every dwelling, for convenience, and had been used in that manner for a century previous. The food of the inhabitants was of the poorest kind, their clothing of the coarsest description, and their education neglected. There are none of the buildings of that time in existence at the present day,—not a vestige of them. The oldest building in the Burgh is the back house of the property, No. 25 High-street, erected in 1594 by Mr. Andrew Knox, minister of the Abbey, on the property that formerly belonged to William Sempill of Third Part. In confirmation of the fact that the fulzie was collected in the streets of Paisley, I may refer to the indictment against the Archbishop of Saint Andrews, Abbot Hamilton, and several monks of Paisley, dated 19th May, 1563, charging them with the crimes of celebrating mass and attempting to restore Popery in the month of April previously, in the Town of Paisley, kirkyard and Abbey-place thereof, and taking auricular confession in the kirk, town, kirkyard, chalmers, barns, *middings*, and killogies thereof. Here we have the Archbishop of Saint Andrews, the legate of the Church of Rome, the Primate of Scotland, the ecclesiastic who had then so recently ruled the Church and State, acting the part of a missionary of his Church, using the little heaps of fulzie on the streets of Paisley for an elevated platform, in addressing a small crowd collected before him, and beseeching the renegades to return to the faith of their fathers, strengthening the waverers with the blessings of Mother Church, and lauding those who had remained firm in the old faith. That street reproach continued for another century, when the population had increased to 900. The Bailies and Council then became ashamed of the appearance of the public streets, and passed the following municipal Act, the first introduction of sanitary reform into the town :—"1661, May 15. Whereas, the Bailies "and Council find, by experience, that people "laying out their foulzie in *middens* at their "door-cheeks, on the foregate, is both unbeseem-"ing, uncomely, and dishonest to the town ; "therefore, they have concluded and ordained "that none hereafter, within the parts, sall mak "their midden at the foregait, but in the back-"sydes, or else lead the same away within forty-"eight hours after they lay it out, under the pain "of ten pounds money *toties quoties*, and this to "be intimated to every family by the officers."

Since writing the foregoing remarks, I have obtained the materials for filling up the gap, or connecting proprietary links of this property. John Dowhill was succeeded by his son, John Dowhill, younger, and the latter obtained a charter on 15th March, 1554, from John, Archbishop of Saint Andrews, abbot of Paslaye, and it is called "the hous or tenement at the gaite heide," that is, the house at the head of the street. In 1573, George Renfrew, John Richie, and Patrick Listoune, succeeded to the property, as heirs of the deceased, John Dowhill, younger. George Renfrew and John Richie sold their shares the same year to John Henrysoune, and he and Patrick Listoune sold the property the following year to Alexander Mure. He obtained a charter from Claud, commendator of Paslay and convent thereof, sealed with the chapter seal of the Abbey, 17th July, 1574, and not subscribed. Alexander Mure sold the tenement to Robert Alexander, burgess, and Janet Mathie, his spouse, in August, 1579, and they obtained a charter from William, commendator of Paslaye, dated 15th January, 1580, and subscribed by him. Claud Hamilton, the com-

Side notes:

Sanitary reform.

Missing links recovered.

Successive proprietors.

Commendators.

mendator, had been forfeited in June, 1579, for concealing and protecting James Hamilton, the assassin of Regent Moray ; and William Erskine of Balgonie, parson of Campsie, a nephew of John, sixth Earl of Mar, had been appointed commendator, and he was forfeited also on 20th August, 1584, for taking part in the raid of Ruthven. A new proprietor of a house generally makes improvements and ameliorations thereon ; and Robert Alexander, on purchasing "Paslay Tak," applied to the Burgh Court and obtained two licenses for liberty "to big twa toofallis to the said dwelling house." A *toofall* is a house laid to the wall of the principal house. On the death of Robert Alexander, the bailies gave sasine to John Alexander, his son and heir, on 15th Dec., 1598. I will now refer to the Pittance Rental (*Paisley Magazine*, page 685), and take the following entry from it :—"The tenement at the nuik "of ye hie gait was ains Jon Dowhills, in anno "1541, and payit, as the Charter bears than, "xxiiijs, now coft be vthers, and perteining "presentlie to John Allexr.   13·4"

The property is very clearly identified with the Charter granted by the Claustral Prior, Henry Baxter, to John Dowhill. John Alexander married Elizabeth Carswell in 1598, and he was admitted a burgess of Paisley in May, 1606, as son and apparent heir of Robert Alexander. Robert Alexander, burgess of Paisley, his father, was owner of property in Causeyside, in which he was infeft along with his wife, Janet Mathie, in 1579. Robert was the son of John Alexander, living in 1558. John was the son of another John Alexander, living in 1541. He was son of another John Alexander, living in 1510. Mr. John Alexander, proprietor of the "Paslay Tak" at the angle of High-street and Saint Mirin's-wnyd, was the owner of several other properties in Paisley, and

Marginal notes:

Licence to erect a toofall.

Pittance Rental.

Alexander family in the 16th century.

moved in the aristocratic circle of society of the day. In the Abbey cemetery there is a venerable tombstone, preserving the names of this worthy gentleman and his estimable lady, bearing the following inscription in *alto-relievo*:—

IOHNE · ALEXANDER · CORDOVNE
ALL·HIS·S

HEIR·LYIS   WALL·HIS·S   JA   VS   R.BVRG
(Shoe-makers' Arms.)   Robert Alexander son to Claud Alexander of Newton

ES · OF · PASLAY · AND · BESSIE · CA

The stone is of a hard black pile, several of which may be seen in the Abbey cemetery, and have all weathered the changes of the atmosphere for the last 200 years. The shoemakers' arms are also cut on the stone,—viz., the crescent knife of the Gentle Craft; and above, the Crown of King Crispin.

Robert Alexander, his eldest son, was born in 1604. He was first apprenticed to Thomas Inglis of Corsflat, writer in Paisley; and after the death of his master, on 27th June, 1622, he finished his apprenticeship with John White, writer in Paisley. Robert Alexander entered on his profession of the law in 1625, and carried on an honourable and successful business. At that period it was customary for gentlemen to have a family arm chair made for their accommodation, containing their armorial bearings, initials of their names, date, and carved foliated and geometrical designs. Mr. Alexander followed the usual rule, and had an arm chair made of oak wood, containing his initals engraved on the top rail, with the date on the next rail, and under these a plain square panel, and the other parts of the chair carved with geometrical designs.

R   A
1 6 2 9

In 1634, Robert Alexander, having married Marion Hamilton, daughter to Claud Hamilton of Black-

Side notes:
Tombstone of John Alexander.

Alexander family of the 17th century.

Robert Alexander, writer,

his

arm-chair,

marriage,

and his
wife's arm-chair.

hole, mentioned in the second lecture, another oak family chair was then made for her, of a similar shape to that of her husband's. Her initials and date were carved in *alto relievo*, the former on the top rail, and the latter on the mid rail, with a square panel between them, containing a carved *cinquefoil* for Hamilton, and the floriated and geometrical carving on the other parts more elaborately executed.

M   H
1   6   3   4

The population of the town that year was 1140. These two venerable family chairs, now 238 years old, are fine specimens of the art of cabinet-making practised in those days ; but whether they are of Paisley workmanship I could not discover ? There was, however, a family of Cochrans who carried on the trade of wrights and turners, owners of one of the properties now occupied by the Paisley Free Library and Museum, contemporaries of Robert Alexander, famed for ingenious cabinet-making and turning of trenchers and cups. The inhabitants of Paisley were in the habit of presenting articles of the latter art to their friends ; and the Town Council, on 22nd December, 1660, concluded that there should be four dozen of trenchers, and one dozen new cups, sent to Sir John Gilmour, and Sir John Fleshour the King's advocate, to move them to continue the town's friends. These chairs are still in good condition, and form very interesting relics in the mansion of Ballochmyle, near Mauchline, the seat of Lieutenant-Colonel Claud Alexander, a lineal descendant of Robert Alexander and Marion Hamilton. Ballochmyle has been made classic ground by the Ayrshire bard, in composing the two heart-stirring songs, "The Braes o' Ballochmyle," and "The Bonnie Lass of Ballochmyle." Ballochmyle belonged to Sir John Whiteford, the

Cabinet-making
and turning.

Presentation of
trenchers and
cups.

descendant of John Whiteford of Whiteford, the first bailie of Paisley, noticed in this lecture, and was purchased from him by Claud Alexander, Esquire, Auditor-General to the East India Company at Bengal, who returned to Scotland and took up his residence on the estate in 1786. One song was written on Miss Maria Whiteford, daughter of the knight, on her leaving home— the sweet home of her youth, ending with the following verse :—

> " But here, alas ! for me nae mair
>   Shall birdie charm, or flowret smile ;
> Fareweel the bonnie banks of Ayr,
>   Fareweel ! fareweel ! sweet Ballochmyle ! "

The other song was written in 1786, on Miss Wilhelmina Alexander, the sister of the Auditor-General, a maiden fair, enjoying the sweet and lovely scenery of the bonnie woods and braes of Ballochmyle, when the poet, musing in a lonely glade, chanced to espy her. Four lines of which I will also quote :—

> " Her look was like the morning's eye,
>   Her ear like nature's vernal smile,
> Perfection whisper'd, passing by,
>   Behold the lass o' Ballochmyle ! "

Miss Alexander was born on Monday, 12th April, 1756, and died at Glasgow on Monday, 5th June, 1843, in the 87th year of her age.

Robert Alexander and Marion Hamilton had two sons,—James, born in 1634, (minister of Kilmalcolm) who died in 1669 ; and Claud, born in 1645, (of Newton) who died in 1703 ; besides two daughters, Janet and Marion. Robert Alexander was appointed Town-clerk of Paisley, at the municipal election in September, 1634, at which time his father-in-law, Claud Hamilton, had been chosen eldest bailie. Robert Alexander was an elder of the Abbey Church, and wrote the deposi-

Marginal notes:

Sir John Whiteford of Ballochmyle, and Claud Alexander of Ballochmyle.

Braes of Ballochmyle.

Bonnie Lass of Ballochmyle.

Children of Robert Alexander's first marriage.

w

Clock for the Cross steeple in 1647.

tion of Margaret Hamilton, the guidwife of Ferguslie, when she was catechised and examined on oath, in her house at Ferguslie, by Mr. Henry Calvert, minister of the Abbey and Commissioner of the Presbytery, on 20th June, 1643, as to her reasons for not attending the Presbyterian Kirk. Mr. Alexander was afterwards appointed clerk of the Presbytery of Paisley, on 27th March, 1645. In 1646-7, he was a Councillor of the Burgh, and it was concluded by a quorum of the Council, on 24th May, 1647 (and I would conclude he was one of them), "that ther sall be ane neu "knock bocht for the toune upon Wednesday next, "the xxvi instant"; and commissioned "John "Vauss and James Alexander to goe in to "Glasgow and buy the ane in the hands of John "Steill." James Alexander was his brother, and several times a Bailie of Paisley. Robert Alexander was appointed a Bailie of Paisley in 1647-8, and on three subsequent occasions.

Bell of the Cross steeple in 1648.

During the term of his office of Bailie, a bell was obtained for the spire or steeple, then at the corner of High-street and Moss-street, bearing the following inscription :—

> " SOLI · DEO · GLORIA .
> CORNELIS · OVDEROCGE · FECIT · EN · D ·
> I · O · ROTTERDAM · ANNO · DOMINI · 1648."

" Glory to God alone. Made by Cornelius Ouderocge, bell-maker and organ-builder, Rotterdam, in the year of our Lord, 1648."

And on the middle of the bell,—

> " FOR · THE · TOWNE · OF · PASLAY."

The bell, after performing its duties to the community for the long space of 215 years, was cracked on 10th March, 1863. This veritable bell, belonging to the period of the Commonwealth of Cromwell, is now in the possession of, and preserved by, Mr. Dundas Smith Porteous, engineer,

Paisley, and for which he paid the price of £26 19s. 7d. That old bell is as finely formed as the best shaped *campanula* (bell flower) that is grown to perfection by an enthusiastic florist, or the blossoms of the indigenous plants called fox glove and blue-bells of Scotland, growing wild in the shelter of our mountain scenery, and beautifully adorning the landscape with their flowers of purple and blue. *

Robert Alexander succeeded to the "Paslay Tak," and he purchased the estate of Blackhouse, near Ayr, in 1648 ; Boghall, in Ayrshire, in 1665 ;

Purchase of Blackhouse and Newton.

---

* EVENTS OF PUBLIC BELLS IN PAISLEY.

I. Cross Steeple Bells.

The first Bell, of 5 cwt. 1 qr. 26 lbs. weight, made by Cornelius Ovderocge, Rotterdam, was originally hung in the old steeple in 1648; and afterwards, in the new steeple in 1758, and cracked on Tuesday, 10th March, 1863, when it was rung on occasion of the nuptial rejoicings at the marriage of the Prince and Princess of Wales. The second Bell, of 7 cwt. 2 qrs. 8 lbs. weight, made by Mears & Co., London, was hung on Friday, 29th May, 1863, and taken down on Tuesday, 6th July, 1869, in consequence of the insecurity of the Steeple.

Cross steeple bells.

II. High Church Steeple Bells.

The first Bell, of 9 cwt. 1 qr. 4 lbs., was hung on Thursday, 2nd May, 1776, and cracked on Tuesday, 1st February, 1820. when it was rung at the accession of King George IV. The second Bell, of 18 cwt. 1 qr. 14 lbs. weight, made by T, Mears, London, was hung on Friday, 8th August, 1823, and cracked on Friday, 27th October, 1865, on being tolled for the funeral of Viscount Palmerston, the Premier. The third Bell, recast from the second Bell (with additional metal), of 21 cwt. 3 qrs. 21 lbs. weight, made by Mears & Stainbank, London, was hung on Monday, 12th February, 1866, and cracked on Friday, 15th December, 1871. The fourth Bell was the Cross Steeple Bell of 1863, temporarily hung on Friday, 19th January, 1872, and taken down on Tuesday, 21st May the same year. The fifth and present Bell, recast from the third Bell, of 21 cwt. 2 qrs. 24 lbs. weight, "James Duff & Son, makers, Greenock, 1872," was hung on Tuesday, 21st May, and rung on the 22nd, the Queen's Birth-day anniversary in Paisley, 1872.

High steeple bells.

and Newton, near Paisley, in 1670; besides a great number of other properties in the Burgh of Paisley. On acquiring the lands of Blackhouse, he took the title "of Blackhouse," and was as proud of it as his father-in-law was of that of Blackhole, for it was inserted in the testing clause of every deed, written by or for him in his business, and can be seen in the contract of sale, dated 3rd May, 1658, between Lord Cochran (Earl of Dundonald), and the Town Council of Paisley, of the superiority of the Burgh by the former to the latter, "writtin be Robert Alexander of blakhous, wrytter in Paislaye." It has been frequently mentioned that this Blackhouse was situated in the parish of Mearns, but that is a mistake. His wife, Marion Hamilton, died in 1648.

Robert Alexander married (2nd) Janet Henderson, daughter and one of the two heiresses of David Henderson, who was the owner of the property now No. 10 High-street, Paisley. They had two sons, Robert, born in 1656 (one of the principal clerks of the Court of Session), and John, born in 1664 (merchant, Carolina). During his lifetime he very considerately conveyed several properties to his younger children, for their help and supplement, "to ane competency of leiving "thereafter;" and, in particular, he granted the present property to his fourth and youngest son, John Alexander. To his second son, Claud Alexander (named after his maternal grandfather, Claud Hamilton of Blackhole), he conveyed the property between the old meal market (now 26 High-street) and Bailie Wallace's house (now 29 High-street), which was formerly noticed in the second lecture, and also his property in Causeyside, called Calseyland, on 24th September, 1669. In 1670, he purchased the lands of Newton, taking the title to himself in liferent, and Claud, his

Margin notes:

Robert Alexander's second marriage, and his children.

Gifting property to them.

second son, in fee. I found an infeftment registered on 16th September, 1675, in favour of Robert Alexander of Blackhouse, Mr. Robert, Claud, and John Alexander, his sons, and John Alexander, oye to the said Robert Alexander of Blackhouse, of the ten-shilling land of Wester Walkinshaw. The oye (named after his maternal grandfather, John Maxwell of Southbar) was the only son of Mr. James Alexander, A.M., ordained minister of Kilmalcolm, in March, 1655, and deprived of his church by the Privy Council, on 1st October, 1662. In 1673, the armorial bearings of Robert Alexander of Blackhouse, and his motto, *Fidem Servia*, were matriculated in the Lyon Register Office. *Fidem Servia* was also his motto to Notarial Instruments. He died in 1687, in the 83rd year of his age.

Matriculation of Alexander arms.

In the ruinous chancel of the famous Monastery of Paisley, there is a flat tombstone with the following initials and armorial representations :—

Tombstone with initials.

R	*(Alexander Arms.)*	A
	1648.	
M	*(Hamilton Arms.)*	H
J	*(Henderson Arms.)*	H

The first initials are those of Robert Alexander of Blackhouse, with the year of erection ; the second initials are those of Marion Hamilton, his first wife ; and the third initials are those of Janet Henderson, his second wife.

In 1807, a tombstone was laid at the right or south side of the lapidary initial and armorial monument to the memory of one of his great-great-grandchildren, sister of Wilhelmina Alexander, and married to her cousin, Claud Neilson, bearing the following inscription :—

Claud Neilson's tombstone.

"LOCKHART ALEXANDER, wife of CLAUD NEILSON,
    died 13th January, 1807, aged 47";

and, twenty years afterwards, there was added

for her husband, another great-great-grandchild :—
> "CLAUD NEILSON, died 6th November, 1825,
>> aged 67."

In 1869, there was engraved on the Neilson tomb-stone an explanatory reading of the *initials*, with additional information :—

New tombstone of Blackhouse.

> "The adjoining grave is the burial-place of
>> ROBERT ALEXANDER
>> of Boghall and Blackhouse,
>> Born 1604,
>> eldest son of JOHN ALEXANDER
>> and ELIZABETH CARSWELL.
>> Also, of his 1st wife,
>> MARION,
>> Daughter of CLAUD HAMILTON.
>> Their 2nd son,
>> CLAUD ALEXANDER of Newton,
>> died in 1703.
>> Also, his second wife, JANET, daughter of
>> DAVID HENDERSON."

Conveyance of Paslay Tak.

On 24th September, 1669, Robert Alexander of Blackhouse, writer, Burgess of Paisley, conveyed to John Alexander, his youngest (4th) son, " All " and Haill that his two tenements of land within " the burgh of Paisley lying contigue and together " of auld called *Pasley Tacks* and the ovenhouse " nooke with houses biggings booths and per- " tinents thereof bounded betwixt the highway " and the tenement of Claud Hamilton on the " east the tenement of umqle William Urie now " belonging to William Young on the south and " west and the high-street on the north parts," under reservation of his life-rent. Wodrow, in his "Church History" (Vol. iv., p. 10), mentions

Transportation of Covenanters to Carolina.

that a great number of persons had been banished to Carolina, and that a contract was entered into with a Walter Gibson, merchant, Glasgow, in 1684, to transport thirty-two of them to Caro-lina and sell them to the planters. Wodrow also says they were harshly treated, their food was of the worst description, and water was scantily given; that the ship's crew were like to mutiny, and *John Alexander* died of thirst, as was thought. At that period, a number of gentlemen left the country from the persecutions of the Government of the day, for the settlement of Carolina. Whether the John Alexander of Wodrow was the son of Blackhouse, and was banished or a voluntary exile, there is no means of knowing; but John Alexander, youngest son of Blackhouse, actually became a merchant in Carolina.

John Alexander returned to Scotland in 1697, and on 7th October of that year he executed his deed of settlement. He designed himself, "John " Alexander, merchant in Carolina, youngest " lawful son to the deceased Robert Alexander of " Blackhouse, writer in Paisley;" and he conveyed the property to "Claud Alexander of Newton, " his brother, second lawful son of the said " Robert Alexander of Blackhouse, in liferent, " and after his decease to Claud Alexander, his " second son, in fee, reserving to the said Claud " Alexander, senior, to alter the destination." The deed was signed at Edinburgh, before "Mr. " Robert Alexander, one of the Clerks of Council " and Session, my brother German," and three other witnesses.

Deed of settlement of John Alexander.

Claud Alexander of Newton was married, in 1677, to Jean Ralston, third daughter of William Ralston of Ralston, who resided at Woodside, in the parish of Beith. William Ralston was one of the party who met at Shuterflat, on 28th November, 1666, under the command of William Mure of Caldwell, although he had made a vigorous attack upon the army of Cromwell. Old Claud Alexander got himself involved in the troubles of the time, and was imprisoned in Edinburgh in 1685, and obtained his liberation on

Claud Alexander of Newton. His marriage

and

imprisonment.

8th August of that year, on giving a bond of a thousand pounds sterling, to live regularly and answer, when called, to anything that is to be laid to his charge. (Wodrow's "Church History," Vol. iv., p. 215.) After the Revolution of 1688, he was, in 1690, appointed a Commissioner of Supply for the County of Renfrew. He was one of the five Commissioners who attested the Poll Tax Rolls of Renfrewshire for the year 1695, and he is entered at page 54, "Claud "Alexander of Newtoune for himself, 4 lib. 6 "sh.; Jean Ralstoune his spouse, 6 sh.; Robert, "Claud, Ursella, and Marion, Alexander's chil- "dren, each 6 sh.; Robert Whyte and Jannet "and Isoball Waylies, servands, each 16 lib. fie, 8 "sh. each, and 6 sh. each general pole." He then resided in Paisley, in the property now No. 87 High-street, which is at the foot of Churchhill and opposite the head of New-street ; but there were neither Churchhill nor New-street in existence in these days. About the same time, the character of Claud Alexander was given by James M'Alpie, Clerk of the Regality Court of Paisley, a poet (whose works the late William Motherwell published in 1828), in the following

Character of Newton.

" ACCROSTICK.

" C lemency becomes a King ;
   L ove, it overcomes all thing ;
   A ge, it brings experience ;
   W ilfulness gives oft offence ;
   D read brings danger att the length.

   A nger was not this man's fate ;
   L oved children dearly, and his mate,
   E ceeding oyrs, voyd of pryde,
   X n like, and meek besyde,
   A ltered nothing by his wealth ;
   N oe nigard was of yt his pelfe,
   E 'er keeping hospitality,
   R emaining still the same to be."

The letter "D" was silent in those days in pronouncing the surname "Alexander," and of course the line for that letter is awanting. It has been frequently alleged that Motherwell was the author of M'Alpie's poems, but the composition of the above accrostic may satisfy any person that Motherwell was not the author of it. Claud Alexander, Robert Sempill, Sheriff at Paisley, and James M'Alpie, his clerk, were chief companions. In 1696, Claud Alexander became a subscriber, and one of the adventurers, for £100 in the joint-stock of the company trading to Africa and the Indies. Young Claud Alexander, the second son, having predeceased his father, old Claud Alexander, in virtue of the faculty he held, conveyed the property to his eldest son, Robert Alexander. This is the Robert Alexander whose name appears on the old tombstone of John Alexander and Bessie Carswell, his great-grandfather and great-grandmother. M'Alpie's Poems African Company.

On the death of Claud Alexander of Newton, his eldest son, Robert Alexander, Writer to the Signet, Edinburgh, succeeded to the "lands of Newton," "Paslay Tak," the property in High-street then called "Aikett's Yard," noticed in the second lecture as claimed by William Stewart and the doomster of the Countess of Mar, and a property in Causeyside called Calseyland. The property in High-street had been purchased by Thomas Inglis of Corsflat; and his only daughter, Anna, a girl of twelve years of age, had been forced by her mother and stepfather to marry William Cunningham of Aikett, a most lamentable circumstance. The property was afterwards called "Lady Aikett's," and she sold it to Robert Alexander of Blackhouse, her father's old apprentice; and it will be found entered in the Rental of Feu-Duties, under the head of Priorscroft, "Robert Alexr, writer, his waist tenement." Robert Alexander of Newton.

x

(*Paisley Magazine*, page 682.) Calseyland was bounded on the north by the lands of Nether Bailzie, and on the west by Saint Mirin's Burn.

Aikett's yard and Calseyland purchased to build a church.

The Town Council of Paisley purchased from Mr. Robert Alexander, Writer to the Signet, Aikett's Yard and Calseyland, on 25th January, 1734, for the purpose of erecting a church for the Burgh of Paisley, to accommodate the increasing population. The Council laid off a street through the centre of Aikett's Yard, crossing Saint Mirin's Burn, and through Calseyland, into Causeyside, leaving a very small space for building on the west side of the new street at Causeyside. The feuing of the steadings in the street for building was commenced in 1734. The street was called "New Street;"

New-street.

and no wonder it was called by that name, for it was the first new street made in Paisley since the village was erected into a Burgh in 1488, —a period of 246 years,—and the street has continued the "New-street" to the present day, although upwards of fifty new streets have been opened since it was named. A part of Calseyland jutted westward, and a lateral street was carried through the centre, which was called "Shuttle-street," after the chief instrument of a weaver, and at a time when almost all the inhabitants were weavers.

Shuttle-street.

The steading at the north-east corner of New-street and Shuttle-street was feued by James Martin, merchant in Paisley, on 12th May, 1735, and he immediately thereafter built a house on the steading, which can be seen at the present time. In digging the foundation for the building, a Gold Lion of King James I. or II. was found. The coin will be about 440 years old, and is in good preservation. It is in possession of Mr. Martin's great-grandson, Archd. Gardner, Esq., of Nether-common, writer in Paisley, who is also pro-

Gold Lion of King James I., found on Calseyland, on the banks of Saint Mirin's rivulet.

prietor of the building. That Gold Lion having become locally connected with New-street and Shuttle-street, and being very rare, I consider it proper to give a description of it,—

GOLD LION OF KING JAMES I. OR II.

Obverse.

IACOBVS DEI GRACIA REX SC

(James, by the Grace of God, King of Scots.)

The Mint mark is the figure of a Crown, and the legend of the King's name is round the margin. Between the words *Iacobus* and *Dei*, there is a *fleur de lis*, and between the words *Gracia* and *Rex*, there is another *fleur de lis*. The Lion Rampant, the Arms of Scotland, from which the gold coins of that monarch obtain their name, is in a lozenge in the centre, within a double tressure, filled with *fleurs de lis*.

Reverse.

SALVVM FAC POPVLVM TVVM A

(Save thy people: so be it.)

The letter *A* is an abbreviation for *Amen*. The Mint mark is a Maltese cross. There is a *fleur de lis* between the Mint mark and the word *salvum*, another between *a* and *l* in *salvum*, two small crosses between *salvum* and *fac*, a *fleur de lis* between *populum* and *tuum*, and another between *A* and the Mint mark. In the centre, a Saint Andrew's cross (with an *I* on the centre) between two *fleurs de lis* enclosed in a sexagon figure, composed of arcs curving towards the centre of the coin, with *fleurs de lis* on the points where the arcs join; and in the curve of each are placed a quatrefoil.

There have been several issues of gold coinage of King James I., who reigned from 1424 to 1437. This particular Gold Lion weighs fifty grains, and is very scarce. I consulted several authors on numismatics, and saw the engravings and read the descriptions of several Gold Lions of that Sovereign. In Lindsay's "Descriptive Catalogue of the Coins of Scotland," it would appear that there is only another coin of King James I. with the same legend and letter A, which is in the British Museum, and I translate the legend,— "*Save thy people. Amen,*"—(page 160, No. 44.)

[Marginal notes:] Obverse and reverse legends. Description of the coin. Rarity of the coin.

The obverse is described on the same page, No. 35. I believe the present Lion is of the highest rarity, and its only known companion is in the British Museum. The legends of some of the other coins on the reverse were, SALVVM FAC POPVLVM TVVM DNE, —*Save thy people, O Lord,*—the letters DNE being a contraction for *Domine.* When or how this Gold Lion was lost, tradition is silent; but it may have been dropped either by Abbot John d'Lychtgow, or his successor, Abbot Thomas Tervas (who built the greater portion of the Abbey towards the year 1451), when they were meditating on the banks of the sainted stream, for they were the most likely persons in these days to be in possession of such a valuable piece of money.

The portion of Calseyland on the east side of New-street, was designed for the church proposed to be erected and churchyard already mentioned; and the portion fronting Causeyside and foot of New-street was sold off in steadings for building. The new church was built in the form of a Grecian cross. The foundation-stone was

laid on 13th May, 1736, and the edifice opened for public worship on 27th August, 1738. It was called the New Church, in contradistinction to the Old or Abbey Church; and next the Laigh Church, after the High Church was built in 1755.

Robert Alexander of Newton, writer to the Signet, married Margaret Alexander, his cousin, daughter of Robert Alexander, Clerk in the Court of Session, third son of Robert Alexander of Blackhouse. The Alexanders of Southbar and Ballochmyle are their lineal descendants, and their genealogy will be found in the histories of Renfrewshire and Ayrshire. On 18th October, 1717, Robert Alexander, lately one of the principal clerks of Council and Session, from his zeal for the glory of God, and out of

Christian charity, love, and affection for the support of his fellow-townsmen, mortified the sum of two thousand marks Scots with the Town Council of Paisley, the interest whereof was to be applied towards the sustentation and maintenance of two old decayed indigent honest persons, man or woman, who have been Burgesses, or children or widows of Burgesses, and have been for a long tract of time residenters and inhabitants within the Burgh, and shall continue to reside therein, free of any scandal, and of good report and deportment. This mortification is better known by the name of "Alexander's Charity." *Alexander's Mortification for indigent persons.*

The "Paslay Tak" property was consumed in the great conflagration, which happened on 2nd June, 1733, noticed in lecture first; and the steading, with its ruins, was sold by Robert Alexander to Robert Maxwell, merchant, then one of the Bailies of Paisley, and David Rodger, wright in Paisley, on 15th November, 1734; and they also acquired the west portion of the *unhouss* or ovenhouse from Francis Ross and Dr. Fulton, on 28th November, 1735. On the former they erected a three-storey house in the Flemish style of architecture, which, with the other three houses to the west, built in the same style of architecture, all with their twin craw-stepped gables to the front, gave the old market place a very ancient looking appearance. They divided the building equally,—David Rodger taking the eastmost half, and Bailie Maxwell the westmost half. The back or ovenhouse portion was divided into two parts,—David Rodger taking the northmost half, and Bailie Maxwell the southmost half. Bailie Maxwell and David Rodger were two of the twenty elders constituting the first session of the New Kirk, afterwards called the Laigh Kirk. *Rebuilding on Paslay Tak, in Flemish style of architecture.*

The erection of new houses on the property of "Paslay Tak," and also on the sites of the *Prosperity of the building trade.*

Laying off New-street.

The ancient Orchard,

and the

lands of Sneddon.

Deepening River Cart by a tax on ale and beer.

other houses that had been consumed by the calamitous fire of 1733, placed the building trade in a prosperous condition, and it flourished afterwards for many years. The New-street and Shuttle-street were both laid off in 1734, to supply the increasing demand for new houses; and it must be admitted that the extending of a town by the building of houses is one of the surest signs of its prosperity. Other trades and businesses in the Burgh were expanding and sharing in the general increasing prosperity of the town. In 1743, the lands of the ancient Orchyard of the abbey, lying on the south side of Causeyside, and north side of Gordon's-lone, containing six acres of land, were divided into several streets, and laid off in stances for building. Other old houses throughout the town that had become waste or dilapidated, were taken down and rebuilt in the intermediate years. The rebellion occurred shortly after the commencement of Orchard-street, but it seems not to have depressed the building trade, for several houses in the old parts of the town bearing the dates of their erection in the ominous figures, "1745," engraved upon them, can be seen at the present day. After the suppression of the Rebellion, by the defeat of the Pretender's army at the battle of Culloden, fought on 16th April, 1746, a tide of prosperity flowed upon Scotland, and particularly in the province of Paisley. In 1749, the lands of Sneddon, on the banks of the River Cart, were next laid off in several streets, and the steadings were instantly taken up for building. The inhabitants, with the view of still further developing the prosperity of the town, directed their attention to the improvement of the navigation of the Cart, by deepening the river; and to raise the ways and means for that desirable object, it was proposed to impose a tax on ale and beer. In 1753, the Town Council of Paisley applied in the 6th session (opened on 11th January, 1753), of the British Parliament which began on the 10th November, 1747, and obtained an Act of Parliament, 26 Geo. II., cap. 96. It is very seldom I have seen that Act noticed ; and, as it is supposed only one copy exists, I will quote more fully from it. The statute is printed in Old English, consists of eleven pages folio, contains eighteen sections, and is entituled, "An Act for laying a duty of two "pennies *Scots*, or one sixth part of a penny "sterling, on every Scots pint of ale and beer "which shall be brewed for sale, brought into, "tapped, or sold, within the town of *Paisley* and "liberties thereof, in the County of *Renfrew*, for "improving the navigation of the River Cart, "and for other purposes."* The ostensible pûr-pose of the statute,—the primary and principal object of the Act,—was the improvement of the river, but a host of other improvements were engrafted on the Act ; and these *other purposes* of the Act might contain the real intention of the promoters. The preamble of the Act proceeds,—

Ale Tax Act.

---

* The other Acts of Parliament passed in reference to the River Cart are the following:—

27 Geo. III., cap. 56, 1787, tituled, "An Act for enabling the Magistrates and Town Council of Paisley to improve the navigation of the River Cart, and to make a navigable cut or canal across the turnpike road leading from Paisley to Greenock."

5th and 6th William IV., cap. 32, 1835,—"An Act to amend an Act for improving the navigation of the River Cart, and for deepening and extending the Harbour of Paisley, in the County of Renfrew."

6 and 7 Victoria, cap. 85, 1843,—"An Act for appointing Trustees for the Creditors of the Burgh of Paisley and other purposes relating to the financial affairs of the said Burgh."

And since the lecture was delivered,

35 and 36 Vict., cap. 32, 1872,—"An Act for regulating the Affairs of the Burgh of Paisley and the River Cart Naviga-tion, and for other purposes."

Acts concerning the River Cart.

"WHEREAS the Town of *Paisley*, in the County of *Renfrew*, carries on a considerable trade in the manufacture of thread and linen cloth, and is situate on the River *Cart*, which falls into the *Clyde*, about four miles below Glasgow ; which said River *Cart* is, by reason of the banks, stones, and rocks therein, scarcely navigable to the Town of *Paisley*, except at the highest spring tides ; and the making of the navigation of the said River practicable and commodious at all times would be a great advantage to the said town : And whereas there is not at present a sufficient Prison, Court-house, School-house for the education of the children, or House of Correction for the punishment of vagrants in the said town, and the shambles are at present in the middle of the town, and a great nuisance to the inhabitants : And whereas the inhabitants of the said town have at their own expense built a new Church, but cannot provide for a Minister to be called thereto, nor can they make the said River navigable, build a Prison, Court-house, School-house, and House of Correction, or remove the shambles to some more commodious place, without the aid of Parliament, the Bailies and Council of the said Burgh of *Paisley* do therefore most humbly beseech your Majesty that it may be enacted ; and be it enacted by the King's most excellent Majesty, by and with the advice and consent of the Lords spiritual and temporal, and Commons, in the present Parliament assembled, and by the authority of the same, that from and after the twenty-fourth day of *June*, in the year of our Lord one thousand seven hundred and fifty three, for the term of thirty-one years, and from thence to the end of the then next Session of Parliament, there shall be laid an imposition or duty of two pennies *Scots*, or one-sixth part of a penny sterling, over and above the duty of excise paid or payable to his Majesty, his heirs and successors, upon every *Scots* pint of ale and beer that shall be either brewed, brought into, tapped, or sold within the said Town of Paisley and liberties thereof : and that the said imposition or duty shall be paid, or made payable, by the brewers for sale, or venders or sellers of all such ale and beer, to the Magistrates and Town Council of the Burgh of Paisley for the time being, who are hereby nominated and appointed Trustees for making the said river navigable, building a Prison, Court-house, School-house, and House of Correction; providing a maintenance for the ministers to be called to the said new Church; and removing the shambles to a more commodious place, and also for putting in execution all other the powers in and by this Act given; and that the money so raised and collected by this Act is, and hereby shall be, vested in the said Trustees; and the same, and every part thereof, shall be paid, applied, and disposed of, or assigned to and for the several uses, intents, and purposes aforesaid, the reasonable charges expended, or to be expended in, about, or by reason of passing this present Act of Parliament, being first deducted."

Providing for ministers of New Church, and removing the shambles.

The other sections in the Act are the following :—

Other sections of the statute.

" 2nd. Officer to be appointed to gauge the vessels.

" 3rd. The Trustees to make orders for the recovery and applying of the duties.

" 4th. Accounts to be kept of all receipts and disbursements.

" 5th. Trustees, with consent of the Overseers, may borrow money on the credit of the duties.

" 6th. Duties, how to be levied and recovered.

" 7th. Beer or ale sold without having paid the duty to be forfeited.

" 8th. Charges of the duty to be ascertained by the vouchers of the officers of excise.

" 9th. Penalty for concealing or embezzling worts, ale, or beer.

" 10th. Persons aggrieved may appeal to the Quarter Sessions.

" 11th. Trustees, with consent of the Overseers, may farm the duty by public roup.

Overseers.

"12th. Overseers of the duty and the receipts and disbursements,—viz.:—

William, Earl of *Glencairn.*
William, Earl of *Dundonald.*
George, Lord *Ross.*
The Honourable *William Ross*, esquire.
William Grant, esquire.
Lord-Advocate for *Scotland.*
Sir *John Maxwell of Pollock.*
Sir *Robert Pollock* of that ilk.
Sir *Michael Stewart* of Blackhall.
William Cunningham of *Craigends.*
William Fliming of *Borrohan.*
William Mure of *Caldwell.*
William M'Dowall of *Castlesemple.*
Boyd Porterfield of *Porterfield.*
John Graham of *Dougulston.*
James Milliken of *Milliken.*
Patrick Crawfurd of *Auchenimes.*
Claud Alexander of *Newton.*
Robert Sempill of *Belltrees.*
The Knight of the Shire.
The Sheriff-Depute for the County of Renfrew."

Meetings of Overseers.

These Overseers were appointed to meet in the Town-house of *Paisley*, on the first Tuesday of August, yearly, to hear complaints.

"13th. Trustees to lay their accounts annually before the Overseers.

"14th. Overseers to appoint which of the public works shall be first undertaken.

"15th. Election of Overseers in room of such as shall die, remove, or refuse to act.

"16th. King's duty not to be prejudiced by any distress hereby to be made.

"17th. Overseers to make satisfaction to the owners of such grounds as shall be damaged by deepening the River, and disputes concerning the same to be settled at the Quarter Sessions.

"18th. Public Act."

Several other Burghs in Scotland obtained

similar Acts of Parliament about the same period, empowering their Councils to levy an impost of two pennies Scots on the pint of ale.

The population of the town at the commencement of the Act, in 1753, was 4195, and the population at the expiry of the Act, in 1784, was 17,560. During that period of thirty-one years, £2500 was levied, which gives an average of £80 yearly. The last year of the impost, from 22nd June, 1783 to 1784, was let to Messrs. Thomas and Matthew Brown, at a rent of £110. The following are the objects to which the revenue was applied :— Application of the tax.

Expenditure.

	£	s	d
1753.—The expense of obtaining the Act and sending two agents to Lond.,	271	1	8
1754.—The building of a Grammar School,	298	0	0
1758.—The building a Prison and Court-house,	1053	7	0
1767.—The building a Flesh Market and Slaughter-house,	965	8	0
1774.—Laid out in deepening the River,	86	6	11
	£2674	3	7

The principal object of the Act was the last attended to, and only one year's revenue of the impost was expended in deepening the river. The Town Council even allowed the representatives of Glasgow to make and erect two dykes or jettees near the mouth of Cart, which obstructed the tidal flow up the Cart, and directed it up the Clyde. The Council demanded damages, and accepted of £150 as compensation for the injury done to their river; but they did not expend a single shilling of that money on the improvement of Cart navigation. Failure in the principal object.

The Grammar School referred to and entered in the above account under the year 1754, is now the house No. 4 School-wynd, and presently occupied as a candle-work. In 1802, a new Grammar School Grammar School buildings.

was erected in Churchhill, bearing the year it was built; and the stone in the previous school, bearing the date 1753, and also the stone with the inscription, "𝔗𝔥𝔢 𝔊𝔯𝔞𝔪𝔞𝔯 𝔖𝔠𝔟𝔦𝔩, 1586," were placed in the Churchhill building. And in 1863 another new Grammar School and Academy was built in Oakshaw-street, and the tablet of 1586 transferred to it.

Prison and Court-house erections.

The Prison and Court-house referred to, under date 1758, was built the previous year, and is referred to in my plan of the district,—"No. 2, the Common Hall." That Prison and Court-house were taken down in 1821, and a new building erected on the site, for additional accommodation to the Saracen's Head Inn. That building was taken down in 1871 by the purchasers, the City of Glasgow Bank, and they have erected a bank on the site, in 1872, for their agency in Paisley, with a clock tower on the circular turn of the building from High-street into Moss-street.

Flesh Market.

In 1753, the Shambles or Flesh Market was situated on the west side of Moss-street, where the house No. 5 of that street has been built. The building of the Flesh Market, referred to in the foregoing account of expenditure, was erected on the east side of the same street, in 1766. The

Front elevation.

front wall, of ashlar work, seventy-two feet long, was in imitation of a two-storey house with blinded windows. The architecture of the building, with its rustic ends and its two large arched rustic doorways, was unmistakably the plan of Bailie John White, stampmaster. The Slaughter-house and yard were situated at the back, and the passage to them was at the north end of the building opposite the School-wynd. The whole traffic to and from the north of the Cross was by Moss-street, then vulgarly called the *Wangaitend*,

Nuisance of cattle continually entering.

and old persons will recollect the awful nuisance in that narrow thoroughfare, by the crying and shouting of butchers and flesher-boys, and the barking of dogs, in driving and beating the cattle into and down the Slaughter-house-lane, and the bellowing of the beasts themselves, sometimes in an infuriated state. The Shambles or stalls were, for many years, occupied by Robert Braid, Robert Speirs, and John Cumming, fleshers. When Gilmour street was opened in 1829, the Slaughter-house was removed to Gockston-road, now called "Bellefield-street." The Moss-street portion of the Flesh Market was sold, in 1835, to Andrew Crawford and Ninian Crawford, manufacturers, 116 Causeyside; and the following year they erected the buildings thereon, called the "Exchange Rooms." A new Flesh Market was erected in Gilmourstreet; but it did not succeed, and was sold to Alexander King, cloth merchant, in 1862, who built a shop and warehouse on the site.

Slaughter-house.

The quantity of ale and beer consumed never yielded a revenue to provide for a minister to the new church; and if it had done so, a strange problem would have required to be solved, namely, —Whether greater evil was committed in the town from the encouragement of ale and beer tippling, to provide a minister's maintenance, or more good promoted in the community by the minister receiving his maintenance from the tax on ale and beer?

Failure of a provision for a minister.

On expiry of the Statute, in 1784, the Town Council applied by Bill to Parliament for a renewal of the Act, with more stringent clauses,— particularly a section including the brewers and vendors *within two miles of the Burgh;* but the inhabitants met the application with a strenuous opposition. The Council obstinately persisted in their plan of taxation, but at last were reluctantly compelled to abandon the Bill, after putting themselves and their opponents to 500 guineas of expenses.

Application for renewal of Ale Tax Act.

Robert Maxwell was, between 1727 and 1749, eight times elected a Bailie of Paisley. Bailie Maxwell conveyed his westmost half of Paslay Tak, and southmost half of his portion of the Ovenhouse, to his only son, John Maxwell, schoolmaster in Paisley, in liferent, and Robert Maxwell his son's son, weaver in Glasgow, in fee,

on 5th November, 1768. Bailie Maxwell executed a testament on 16th January, 1769, in favour of his son, John Maxwell, of all his household plenishing and furniture, and sums of money under certain exceptions, "with my whole mer-
"chant and shop goods of any kind,—such as
"ropes, naills, weir pots, lead, &c." That short enumeration, gives an idea of the merchandise carried on by the Bailie at the Cross of Paisley, which seems to have been that of an ironmonger.

The exceptions were the following bequests :—To his daughter, Jean Maxwell, wife of John Hart, late merchant in Paisley, his large press, standing in the high fore-room, then possessed by Miss Kibble, together with his wife's large Bible.   To his daughter, Janet Maxwell, relict of Robert Maxwell of West-brae, his wife's chest, standing in his high back-room, possessed by Miss Kibble. To his daughter Margaret Maxwell, spouse of John Craig, merchant in Paisley, a four-square table in her own possession, and the new and best lint-wheel, and his arm-chair in his kitchen. And to Elizabeth Maxwell, his daughter, spouse of William Alexander in Campbeltown, the works of Mr. John Flavel, in two large folio volumes. Bailie Maxwell died before 1772, and the place of his sepulture is pointed out by a headstone in the Laigh churchyard, with the following inscription : "1750. This is the burial-place appointed for Robert Maxwell, merchant." The foregoing bequests give an idea of the will of a respectable merchant and Bailie of Paisley a century ago, whose four daughters were married to respectable merchants of the day.

John Hart, husband of Jean Maxwell, was pro-proprietor of part of the lands of Ferguslie, situated on the south side of the road, which he called *Hartston ;* while the lands of Ferguslie to the west of Hartston were purchased by George Millar, merchant, High-street, and he called them Millarston ;—and all these lands, with the exception of three steadings, now belong to Thomas Coats, Esq. of Ferguslie. John Hart was also owner of other properties in Paisley, and the lands of Kilbowie in West Kilpatrick. He was elected a Bailie of Paisley in 1745 and 1747, and he was one of the founders of the " Society for the Reformation of Manners," in 1757. In 1758, he failed in £4360 12s. 4d.—Robert Maxwell, husband of Janet Maxwell, was the fourth and youngest son of Gavin Maxwell of Castlehead. He feued his lands of West-brae on the east side of Lonewells, and north side of Wellmeadow and West-brae, in 1751. He was elected a Bailie of Paisley in 1755. His only son, Gavin Maxwell of West-brae, was a very pompous little man, and was appointed one of the lieutenants of the Paisley first regiment of volunteers, raised in 1803. He was the chief objector, in 1808, to the taking down of that piece of stunted architecture, called the Almshouse Steeple, better known as the "wee Steeple," built in 1724. William Craig, surgeon, another Paisley poet, on that occasion penned a few lines on " The Rise and Fall of the Little Steeple," the last four lines of which I will quote :—

" When frugal rulers, at whose angry frown
　　Both church and steeple must come tumbling down,
　　For public good bade sound my dying knell,
　　Gaun lost the combat and the steeple fell."*

---

* Mr. Craig was born in Paisley on the 11th June, 1789, and died 13th January, 1829. Several of his pieces appeared in

[Margin notes:]
John Hart of Hartston.

Robert Maxwell of West-brae.

Fall of the Wee Steeple.

William Craig, surgeon.

John Craig, merchant.

Gavin Maxwell was a wealthy gentleman; but was always afraid he would become an inmate of the Poorhouse. He died suddenly in 1811. He was succeeded by his sisters, Elizabeth Maxwell (who died 22nd December, 1834, aged eighty-four years), wife of William Patison, Master of Works, before noticed, and Agnes Maxwell (Mrs. M'Lean), and his nephew, Mr. Nathaniel Stevenson, writer, Glasgow.—John Craig, husband of Margaret Maxwell, was a merchant in Old Sneddon-street, Paisley, and resided in the property No. 11 of that street, on which a new house has been erected by Mr. James M'Ghee. He left two sons, John and Robert, and two daughters. His daughter, Janet, married George Bell, auctioneer, afterwards merchant in Glasgow; and after the death of her youngest brother, Robert Craig, in 1835, she succeeded to the Sneddon property. One of her sons was the late Mr. David Bell, merchant, proprietor of the Queen's Rooms, Glasgow. John Craig, jun., was a writer in Paisley, who married Jean Gibb, daughter of John Gibb, innkeeper, and owner of No. 13 High-street, Paisley, and Serjeant's Acre, between Dar-

Coaches between Paisley and Glasgow and Greenock.

skeith Wood and Ferguslie. In 1782, Mr. Gibb ran coaches between Paisley and Glasgow four times a day each way,—fares, 1s.; and a diligence between Paisley and Greenock twice a week each way,— fares, 4s. John Craig, writer, died in 1802. John Gibb died on 7th October, 1836, aged ninety-two; and his daughter, Mrs. Craig, died on 9th October, 1857, aged eighty-eight years.—Wm. Alexander,

William Alexander, merchant.

---

the "Scottish Minstrel" of R. A. Smith, and the pages of the local papers. In 1798, his father, Robert Craig, purchased the old meal mercat of Paisley, built in 1665, and he made it fall in 1799, and erected the present house of three storeys, where he carried on the business of a provision dealer for a quarter of a century. The house now belongs to Mr. John Gibb, hosier.

husband of Elizabeth Maxwell, was a merchant in Ferguslie, and on 13th May, 1755, he purchased from John Hart part of the lands of Hartston. He afterwards went to Campbeltown, and returned to Paisley. In 1792, he conveyed the property to his son, William Alexander, jun., merchant in Antigua. On the death of the son, he was succeeded by his brother, Archibald Alexander, bleacher, in 1812. His eldest son is William Alexander, writing-master, Paisley, whose poetic effusions frequently appear in the poet's corner of the local newspapers, and occasionally in the London papers. Mr. John Flavell, whose works were bequeathed to Mrs. Alexander, was an eminent non-conformist divine, who died on 26th June, 1691.

John Maxwell, the life-renter of the subjects, succeeded his father about 1772, and died in 1787. The half that belonged to Bailie Maxwell was next acquired by Mr. Alexander Weir, merchant at the Cross of Paisley, and tenant of the premises, from Robert Maxwell, the grandson, on 26th November, 1787. Mr. Weir was born at Parkhead of Inverary, on 15th October, 1742, and afterwards educated in one of the parish schools. He displayed some ability at school, and the teacher evinced an interest in the education of his pupil. When a member of the Duke's family visited the school, the teacher took the opportunity of parading little Alexander before them, to give a favourite recitation. The boy was sent to the Lowlands when he was eight years of age, on the occasion of his father's second marriage. In course of time he came to Paisley, and adopted it as his future residence. He commenced and carried on the business of a cloth-merchant for several years, in the premises which he had purchased, both before and after the purchase. Mr. Weir was a person of more than ordi-

Marginal notes: Alexander Weir, merchant,　his education,　and　residence.

z

Alexander Weir, merchant.

nary talent and intelligence, and he made himself conspicuous, from the deep interest he took in the various social, religious, and political movements which engrossed the attention of his fellow-townsmen. On 24th September, 1774, he was married to Jane, eldest daughter of William Wilson, of Hurlet, and sister of the late John Wilson, of Thornley. In religion, Mr. Weir was a Presbyterian, belonging to the Established Church. He was ordained an elder of the High Church, under the ministry of Dr. Muir; but worshipped in the Middle Church during the ministry of the Rev. John Snodgrass, D.D. The churches in Paisley were at that time well attended, and the Middle Church was generally crowded to the doors. Dr. Snodgrass was the first minister of the Middle Church, inducted on 19th December, 1781, and died 22nd June, 1797, in the 56th year of his age and 27th of his ministry. He was a very popular divine, and lectured frequently on the Apocalypse. Mr. Weir, having come from the Highlands, took considerable interest in the Gaelic population of the town, and

Building of the Gaelic Church

was chiefly instrumental in promoting the erection of the building in Oakshaw-street, Paisley, having a tablet in front, inscribed

GAELIC
CHAPEL
MDCCXCIII

where the Highlanders residing in Paisley and neighbourhood might worship. Mr. Weir purchased the ground from James Wallace of Caversbank, and obtained a disposition in his own name on 6th May, 1793; and he executed a conveyance in favour of Trustees, containing the constitution of that chapel of ease, on 26th April, 1795. In politics, Mr. Weir was a Liberal—a Democrat, at a time when it required some courage to avow their principles, and wear the colours of his class. Notwithstanding these opinions, Mr. Weir was so much respected for the support he gave to every movement for the advancement of the social comfort and morality of the people, that the Tory Council of 1781 elected him a Town Councillor. In 1775 he became a member of the Society for the Reformation of Manners, and in 1793 he was elected president. Mr. Weir was one of the witnesses to the indenture of Alexander Wilson, afterwards poet and ornithologist, when he was apprenticed to the trade of a weaver, on 31st July, 1779; and Mr. Weir was also one of the two persons who dined with Burns, the Ayrshire poet, when he visited Paisley. Mr. Weir was possessed of a great amount of natural sagacity, and was frequently selected to act as referee or umpire in cases of dispute between parties. Several years before his death he retired from business, and took up his residence at Thornley, where he died on 24th July, 1819, in the 77th year of his age. His relict, Jane Wilson, died 14th March, 1825. Mr. Weir, when he was in Edinburgh, in the year 1788, attending the General Assembly as a ruling elder, purchased and brought home the first umbrella seen in Paisley. It was originally covered with oiled cloth, and it is now covered with cotton cloth. This venerable umbrella of bygone times is in good condition, considering its age, and is in the possession of Mr. John Lorimer, his grandson. Many thousands of umbrellas must have been worn out in the Burgh since that, the first one, was brought into the town, which is unquestionably the oldest umbrella in Paisley. Mr. Weir sold the property in 1798, and became tenant of Cardonald, where he erected a grain mill.

Marginal notes:

Alexander Weir, merchant.

Indenture of Alex. Wilson, poet.

Dining with Robert Burns, poet.

First umbrella in Paisley.

John Watt, merchant in Paisley, acquired the
subjects on 18th October, 1798 ; and when he re-
sold them, he was then residing in Glasgow.
John Henderson, merchant in Paisley, next bought
the property on 9th June, 1813, and there carried
on his business of a cloth merchant. His son,
Andrew Henderson, now merchant in Hamilton,
who succeeded to the property in 1840, sold it on
21st May, 1849, to Mr. William Wotherspoon of
Maxwellton House. Mr. Wotherspoon pulled
down the Flemish twin gable and west portion of
the house in 1849, and erected the present two-
storey house on the site, which is presently occupied by Mr. William M'Intyre, stationer, Cross.
The back portion of this part of "Paslay Tak"
is presently used by Mr. M'Intyre as sub-collector
of "Government Tax." On 2nd July, 1869, the
dismantling of the falling Cross Steeple com-

menced, by the removal, first, of the hands of
the clock, and then the clock itself, which had
been made by James M'Wattie, wright and clockmaker, Causeyside-street, Paisley, in the year
1776. The committee of the Town Council
selected, and Messrs. Wotherspoon and M'Intyre
generously offered, to allow a public clock to be
erected on their premises ; and on the 16th July,

1870, it was put up by being projected from the
pediment. The clock case is made of cast-iron, in
the form of a drum, with two horologes, and
illuminated with gas. Bailie Richard Watson,
editor of the *Paisley Herald*, was the convener of
the committee for obtaining the time-piece at the
Cross ; and although many a joke was made on
the occasion respecting the size and appearance of
the new public clock, the inhabitants are very
much indebted to the Bailie for persevering, and
supplying one of the greatest wants that the
market-place of Paisley had experienced during
the last three hundred years. Abbot George

Schaw, the founder of the Burgh, erected the market cross of Paisley in 1488, in a position to be seen east and west; and Bailie Watson, with equal sagacity, had his market clock erected in a similar manner, by which his name will be handed down to posterity as a public benefactor.*

John Rodger succeeded his father, David Rodger, in the eastmost half of *Paslay Tak*, and southmost half of the *Ovenhouse*. He was succeeded by his son in the one half thereof, *pro indiviso*, in 1759. He sold it to William Russell, in Caldcoats, in 1775; and James Russell, his son, succeeded in 1790. John Rodger, in fulfilment of the wish of his father, conveyed the other *pro indiviso* half to his brother, William Rodger; and the latter was succeeded by his son, William Rodger, in 1780.

John Johnston, thread maker in Paisley, acquired both *pro indiviso* halves from James Russell and William Rodger, in 1795 and 1797. John Johnston had also acquired several other properties in Paisley. He resided in the property No. 97 High-street, now belonging to Messrs. Parlane, booksellers. He died suddenly in 1797, unmarried, and was succeeded by his brother, Hugh Johnston, seaman on board His Majesty's Ship of war, called the "Atlas," who afterwards became a weaver in Paisley. Hugh Johnston commenced immediately to dispose of the properties his brother had by industry acquired, and the first one he sold was the property at the Cross. He died in 1803.

Mr. Alexander M'Alister, merchant, Cross, Paisley, next acquired the subjects on 25th October, 1797, and carried on business in the shop

Marginal notes: John Rodger. John Johnston. Alexander M'Alister.

---

* On 31st July, 1872, the Town Council erected a public clock in the clock tower of the City of Glasgow Bank, at the Cross, which was fitted up by John Lyle, clockmaker, Paisley, at the cost of £34 18s. 6d.

on the premises. In 1801-4 and 1813 he was elected a Bailie of Paisley. About 1817, he and his sons commenced business as manufacturers in Gauze-street; and about 1818, he built a four-storey house on the Ovenhouse part of the subjects. He died in 1843, in the 81st year of his age. Part of the four-storey house was occupied by John Neilson, printer, in 1819; and Mr. Neilson continued in business till 1850, when he removed to Glasgow. The *Paisley Advertiser,* the first newspaper published in Paisley, was printed in that latter building by Mr. Neilson, and the first number was sent forth to the world on 9th October, 1824, and the last on 27th July, 1844. He also printed the *Weavers' Magazine* in 1819, the *Paisley Magazine* in 1828, and the *Renfrewshire Magazine* in 1847. His father, John Neilson, commenced the printing business in Paisley in 1788, and between father and son, they were sixty-two years in the trade. During these six decades they printed a very great number of local publications, a catalogue of which would be a very interesting list, if any Bibliopolist would undertake the contribution.

This portion of the property was purchased by Robert M'Kechnie, doctor of medicine in Paisley, on 26th June, 1829, at the price of £920. Dr. M'Kechnie was a skilful surgeon, and early arrived at the head of the medical profession in Paisley, a position which he maintained till his death on 9th June, 1853, in the 74th year of his age. In the year 1803, he received the appointment of assistant-surgeon to the first regiment of volunteers raised in Paisley that year. Mr. Robert M'Kechnie, manufacturer in Paisley, his second son, succeeded to the property on his father's decease, and he has sold it to the Commissioners of Police for the improvement.

The front property, or east half of Paslay

Marginal notes:

Printing of first newspaper in Paisley.

Robert M'Kechnie, M.D.

Tak, was bought on 15th May, 1829, by *Robert Hendry, druggist in Paisley,* and his trustees have sold it to the Commissioners of Police, supposed by the public for erection of a steeple at the Cross, in lieu of the Cross Steeple taken down in 1871. It is now very questionable whether money will be squandered in the erection of a steeple by itself, without being in connection with Municipal Buildings or a Town Hall. It will be a very difficult matter to obtain a good central site of sufficient extent to combine Municipal Buildings, Town Hall, and a Steeple. A proper site is of the greatest consequence; but some economical people would place them in an improper situation, to save £500 on the purchase of a superior site, never taking into consideration that the expense of building on either a good or a bad site is the same.

Site for new Cross Steeple.

I have now concluded my investigations regarding the Old Places, the Old Families, and the Olden Times of the Ancient Village and Burgh of Paisley, in the district through which the spacious opening from the Cross to Causeyside will be formed. When the Philosophical Society asked me to read a paper on the subject, I had no idea that the old ground would turn out so fertile, and produce a course of four lectures. In commencing each lecture, it fortunately happened that the original Charters of Laŭbhouss, Blakhole, Anhouss, and Paslay Tak, were in existence, which gave me authentic data to begin with; and, according to the auld Scots proverb, "A gude beginning makes a gude ending." Not the smallest aid could be obtained from either direct or conflicting tradition; because it had not been handed down, or had sunk into oblivion. The facts adduced have been fortified with names and dates, the backbone and bulwark of history, and I verified these by several hundreds of references to the original documents themselves. The time

Concluding remarks regarding Old Places, Old Families, and Olden Times.

Proofs.

allowed for preparation was very short for a subject shrouded in obscurity, and embracing a period extending backwards 440 years.

The various industries now carried on in town have added materially to the prosperity of the Burgh, and enabled the Commissioners of Police to purchase valuable properties to open up the communication with two of the most ancient places in Paisley, projected and attempted to be carried out for the last seventy years. The spacious opening which I have marked SAINT MIRIN PLACE on the ground plan, will be a vast improvement to the town. The present Saint Mirren-street is only sixteen feet wide, and the proposed SAINT MIRIN PLACE will be fifty feet wide at the Cross, one hundred and ten feet wide at the centre, and one hundred and sixty feet wide at Causeyside, which will make it of a triangular form. The latter width may be partly very properly occupied with a Statue of Saint Mirin, the tutelary Saint of Paisley; or Abbot George Schaw, the founder of the Burgh; or a celebrated native poet, to please the sons of song and the musical population; or a popular civic dignitary of the Burgh, to gratify the burgesses. Since the improvement has been effected, I trust the present prosperity will go on progressing, and that other contemplated improvements will follow in due succession.

In closing, I have to thank my auditors, who have so patiently and attentively listened to the several lectures respecting their native town.

DAVID SEMPLE.

Margin notes: SAINT MIRIN PLACE. — Place for erection of a statue.

In Memoriam
JAMES JAMIESON LAMB.

Born, 24th October, 1817;
Died, 27th September, 1872.

In the 55th Year of his Age.

S AD at heart I feel, in writing this small tribute
  of respect to the memory of the Convener of
the Antiquities Section Committee of the Paisley
Philosophical Society.   The late Mr. LAMB, in that
capacity, officiated as Chairman at the first of the
foregoing lectures, and before they have finally
passed through the press, he has passed away.

Mr. LAMB belonged to a family of four genera-
tions of Architects—grandfather, father, himself, and
son, all having adopted that honourable profession.
The late Mr. LAMB received a liberal education ;
and in pursuing his studies he acquired a taste for
books, and collected one of the largest and best
selected libraries of ancient and modern authors,
in the various branches of science, literature, and
art, in the West of Scotland.   He also cultivated
the study of Antiquities, and frequently visited distant places to examine the works of bygone ages.
Lectures and Lecturers afforded Mr. LAMB considerable pleasure and delight, and he was for many
years the chief promoter of several courses of these
elevating and instructive enjoyments in his native

A *

Convener of an-
tiquities section,

and

Chairman at first
lecture.

Family of archi-
tects.

Study of antiqui-
ties.

Lectures and
lecturers.

town, and securing the services of gentlemen emin-
ently qualified for delivering these intellectual treats.
My esteemed departed friend became deeply inter-

Publication of foregoing lectures.

ested in the printing and publication of the preceding lectures, and he perused several of the proof
sheets that had been printed. Little did I think
when I met him on Tuesday evening leaving the

Usual health, and sudden demise.

gate of the Free Library in his usual health and
strength, again entrusted by the Lecture Committee
with the responsibility of engaging distinguished Lecturers for the ensuing season, that on the Friday
morning following I would have the melancholy
fact to record, — Lamb is dead !

Numismatic collection.

Mr. LAMB also devoted a large portion of his
time to Numismatics, and he has collected and left
a rich and valuable cabinet of ancient and modern
coins, medals, and bronzes. He was an ardent

The drama.

admirer of the Drama, and his watchword was
Shakspere. Sculpture and Painting engaged his
artistic taste. Poetry and Music were favourite
studies. He made a magnificent Autographical col-

Collection of autographs.

lection, illustrated with engraved and photographic
busts, and enlivened with short memoirs of the
Writers of the Autographs. He was a member of
almost all the local incorporations and institutions,
and was often elevated to the Directorate. He was

Civic and masonic offices.

a Bailie of the Burgh, a Justice of the Peace for the
County, and a high dignitary in the Masonic Brother-
hood. His natural talents, combined with his extensive knowledge derived from standard works and

Literary pursuits.

high-class periodicals, led him into literary pursuits ;
and many serials and the local papers have been
embellished with well-written articles emanating

from his prolific and versatile pen. His conversations with Lecturers, and contributions to the Press, made him acquainted with many of the living literary celebrities, either from personal interview or written correspondence. His genial and warm-hearted disposition secured him many friends. He was an intellectual and intelligent gentleman of high literary attainments, and much respected in the community. In his business he gave excellent advice and counsel to tradesmen; and in his profession I will refer to two of his latest specimens of Architecture,—the Town Hall of Johnstone, and the Municipal Buildings of the Royal Burgh of Renfrew, —in which his eldest son and successor, Mr. James Barr Lamb, was associated. *Specimens of architecture.*

From the time Mr. LAMB was seized with the fatal malady, he gradually sunk; and after a short illness of forty-eight hours the silver cord was loosed. Mr. LAMB has left a widow and eight children to mourn his loss, and the community sympathise with them in their sudden bereavement. Mr. LAMB's tall conspicuous figure will never be seen again on the streets, his industrious pen has fallen from his hand, and his well known voice is hushed for ever. *Short illness.* *Sympathy for Mrs. Lamb and children.*

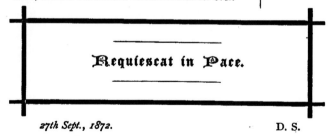

Requiescat in Pace.

27th Sept., 1872. D. S.

INDEX.

B *

J. AND J. COOK, STEAM PRINTERS, PAISLEY.